The Teachers & Writers Guide to
William Carlos Williams

The Teachers & Writers Guide to
William Carlos Williams

Edited by Gary Lenhart

Teachers & Writers Collaborative
New York

Library of Congress Cataloging-in-Publication Data

The teachers & writers guide to William Carlos Williams / edited by
    Gary Lenhart.
        p.   cm.
    Includes bibliographical references.
    ISBN 0-915924-57-9 (alk. paper)
    1. Williams, William Carlos, 1883–1963--Study and teaching.
    2. English language--Rhetoric--Study and teaching. 3. Creative
    writing--Study and teaching. 4. Academic writing--Study and
    teaching. I. Lenhart, Gary.
    PS3545.I544Z893 1998
    811'.52--dc21

Teachers & Writers Collaborative
5 Union Square West
New York, New York 10003-3306

Cover and page design: Christopher Edgar

Front cover image: William Carlos Williams's 1914 self-portrait is reprinted by permission of the Department of Special Collections, Van Pelt-Dietrich Library Center, University Libraries, University of Pennsylvania.

Printed by Philmark Lithographics, New York, N.Y.

Acknowledgments

This book would not have been possible without the help of Daniel Allman, the rights and permissions director of New Directions. Thanks also to Tim Davis of New Directions for his assistance; to Paul Mariani, for swiftly responding to our queries; to John Pollack of the Van Pelt Library at the University of Pennsylvania, for permission to use the self-portrait by William Carlos Williams that appears on this book's cover; and to Bob Rosenthal and the Allen Ginsberg Trust, for permission to reprint Allen Ginsberg's "An Exposition of William Carlos Williams's Poetic Practice."

This publication was made possible, in part, through support from the Witter Bynner Foundation for Poetry and the National Endowment for the Arts.

Teachers & Writers programs are made possible, in part, through support from the National Endowment for the Arts, the New York State Council on the Arts, and the New York City Department of Cultural Affairs.

T&W also thanks the following foundations, corporations, and individual donors: Anonymous Donor, Apple Computer, Inc., Bell Atlantic Foundation, Bertelsmann USA, The Bingham Trust, Booth Ferris Foundation, Bronx Borough President and City Council, The Bydale Foundation, The Louis Calder Foundation, The Cerimon Fund, The Chase Manhattan Foundation, Consolidated Edison, Simon and Eve Colin Foundation, Charles E. Culpeper Foundation, The Dammann Fund, Heavy D and the Universal Music Group, Marvin Hoffman and Rosellen Brown, J. M. Kaplan Fund, Lannan Foundation, Morgan Stanley Foundation, M&O Foundation, Manhattan Borough President and City Council, National Broadcasting Company, Inc., The New World Foundation, New York Times Company Foundation, Henry Nias Foundation, Overbrook Foundation, Thomas Phillips and Jane Moore Johnson Foundation, Prudential Foundation, Queens Borough President and City Council, Mel and Barbara Ringel, Maurice R. Robinson Fund, Helena Rubinstein Foundation, the Scherman Foundation, Steven Schrader and Lucy Kostelanetz, Alison Wyegala (in memory of Sergio Guerrero), and T&W's many individual members.

Permissions

The following poems by Williams Carlos Williams are reprinted by generous permission of New Directions Publishing Corporation: "January Morning," "The Red Wheelbarrow," "Nantucket," "10/22," "Stormy," "Poem" ('As the cat'), "Good Night," "The Hurricane," "Danse Russe," "The Young Housewife," "The Thinker," "Portrait of a Lady," "This Is Just to Say," "The Locust Tree in Flower" (versions 1 and 2), "Between Walls," "The Great Figure" (versions 1, 2, and 3), "To a Solitary Disciple," "Portrait of a Woman in Bed," "The Last Words of My English Grandmother," "Young Woman at a Window," "Proletariat Portrait," "To a Poor Old Woman," "The Hunters in the Snow," "Peasant Wedding," excerpts from *Spring and All*, "Young Sycamore," "The Jungle," and "Impromptu: The Suckers." Reprinted from *The Collected Poems of William Carlos Williams: Volume I*, edited by A. Walton Litz and Christopher MacGowan ©1986, and from *The Collected Poems of William Carlos Williams: Volume II*, edited by Christopher MacGowan © 1988.

Kenneth Koch's essay is adapted from his book *Rose, Where Did You Get That Red?*, published by Vintage Books (copyright © 1973, 1990). Reprinted by generous permission of the author and the publisher.

Charles Demuth's *The Figure 5 in Gold* is from The Metropolitan Museum of Art, The Alfred Stieglitz Collection, 1949 (49.59.1) and is reproduced by permission of The Metropolitan Museum of Art.

In memoriam
Robert T. H. Davidson

Table of Contents

Preface: Why William Carlos Williams?

by Gary Lenhart

In 1991, Teachers & Writers published a guide to Walt Whitman to mark the centenary of that great American poet's death. Today Whitman's worldwide popularity makes it easy to forget that many American poets in the first part of this century considered him an embarrassment. His sympathies were too broad, his diction uncouth, his philosophy eclectic, his optimism vulgar. William Carlos Williams stands out among the poets of the modernist generation for his ardent embrace of Whitman's democratic aims and inclusive American idiom. Like Whitman, Williams celebrates the New World for its free-spirited variety and revels in the carnival of its inventive voices. In an essay titled "America, Whitman, and the Art of Poetry," Williams wrote that American verse must be "free to include all temperaments, all phases of our environment, physical as well as spiritual, mental and moral. It must be truly democratic, truly free for all." So it is appropriate that in this series, designed to encourage imaginative writing by a democratic range of students, one of these guides be devoted to Williams.

But there's an even more compelling reason for this book. Reading the poems and stories of William Carlos Williams makes almost anyone want to write. He wrote poems that elementary students respond to immediately, that have bracing effects on the poetic maunderings of the dreamiest adolescent, and that refresh and inspire poets who have been writing for many years. Because Williams's writing is direct, unencumbered, and energetic, it inspires readers to attempt their own poems and stories. I have had students who found Williams's work puzzling, superficial, peculiar, sensational, even crazy, but I have never known students to feel intimidated by it. Williams's voice is not that of an oracle or authority instructing us how we should feel, but that of a family member or neighbor challenging us to respond as we would in conversation. Williams wrote that "the thing that stands eternally in the way of really good writing is always one: the virtual impossibility of lifting to the imagination those things which lie under the direct scrutiny of the senses, close to the nose." That's why the poems written by second and third graders in this book dazzle by their "direct scrutiny," and why Williams

is a desirable model for high school and college students often in full
flight from the testimony of their senses.

William Carlos Williams was a first-generation American, born in
the same New Jersey town that he lived in all his life. His English father
and Puerto Rican mother spoke Spanish at home. Though he decided
while a student at the University of Pennsylvania that he wanted to pur-
sue poetry, he took his degree in medicine, and returned to his hometown
to practice pediatrics and obstetrics. There he built a practice among
the poorer members of the community, and learned to make poems and
stories in a language that came, as he put it, from "the mouths of Pol-
ish mothers."

He published his first book of poems in 1909, and another one four
years later. In 1913, at the age of thirty, Williams was sparked by the
avant-garde Armory Show in New York City. The effects on his writing
were dramatic. He turned from the groping Keatsian imitations of his
first two books to the romance of modernism. He became an active
member of the group of avant-garde artists that gathered around *Others*
magazine and Alfred Stieglitz's art gallery, and suddenly began to write
poems that were unprecedented and original.

He visited New York City often, frequented Greenwich Village par-
ties, and was on friendly terms with many of the writers and painters of
his time. He spent two extended sabbaticals in Europe, principally in
Paris, where through his friends Ezra Pound and Robert McAlmon he
met Ernest Hemingway, James Joyce, Gertrude Stein, and many French
writers and artists. Yet most of his own books were issued in small editions that were poorly distributed. Most often, like Whitman, he under-
wrote them (until New Directions began to publish Williams when he
was in his mid-fifties).

Throughout, Williams remained in pursuit of a new measure to
accommodate the speech patterns of American English. Sometimes he
talked about a "variable foot," sometimes the "American idiom," but
always to the same point, "that we here must listen to the language for
the discoveries we hope to make." He emphasized repeatedly that American was a new language, with its own music and metric. To understand
what he meant, we have only to listen to prominent American actors
contest with iambic pentameter in a film version of *Julius Caesar*. Better yet, listen to the mesmerizing recording of W. H. Auden reciting "In

Memory of W. B. Yeats," then to Williams's excited nasal recital of any of his own poems.

Williams's writing career was so long and varied and his energy so great that separate volumes could be devoted to teaching his poems, fiction, nonfiction, and plays. In this book we have included essays about many aspects of his writing. Penny Harter writes about using Williams's long poem *Paterson* to free high school students to write about their own surroundings; Bob Blaisdell and David Surface show how Williams's short stories shake up our expectations; Chris Edgar considers the lessons for writers in Williams's pioneering stabs at reviving American history; and Jordan Davis writes about the liveliest baby in literature, described by Williams in the first pages of his novel *White Mule.* In line with Williams's close and lifelong relation to painting, Barbara Flug Colin and Sally Cobau discuss the use of visual arts as prompts for student writing. We are privileged to listen in as Allen Ginsberg walks his students through a volume of Williams's poems, and are dazzled by the responses to Williams that Kenneth Koch elicits from elementary school students. To demonstrate the virtues of Williams's poems, Julia Alvarez composes and distributes to students her paraphrases of them. Mary Edwards Wertsch and Peggy Garrison write about teaching the short imagist poems for which Williams is justly famous. To understand better the poet's view of things, Reed Bye looks closely at Williams's advice "To a Solitary Disciple." Charles North uses the serial images of "January Morning: A Suite" to show how students may build longer poems from brief sightings. Ron Padgett discusses a few gems in the Williams *Collected* that are often overshadowed by plums and wheelbarrows. Bill Zavatsky tells us what he has learned from listening to recordings of Williams's voice and where we may go to listen too. I talk about my favorite sure-fire poetry exercise (modeled upon two persona poems by Williams) and my humbling attempts to challenge students with two of his more offbeat poems.

You will find this book full of ideas for writing and for teaching writing. Some readers mistakenly interpret Williams's phrase "no ideas but in things" to mean that he opposed ideas. Rather, he felt that ideas should not precede events, but arise from particular occasions. The ideas that we present here were developed in many different classrooms. Because these ideas worked in those contexts, we believe many of them will strike a chord in you and your students.

Julia Alvarez

Rewriting William Carlos Williams
(For a Good Cause)

Wherever he is, I hope William Carlos Williams forgives me. I have used his poems for what I hope he would consider a good cause. But who knows, maybe when I get to wherever he is, I'll find he's donated my poems to the making of fires in the circle of hell reserved for writing teachers who rewrite the poems of great poets in order to prove a point about poetry.

Yes, I rewrite William Carlos Williams, but let me say right from the start that I am not trying to improve upon his poems. Their bright clarity, sharp concrete imagery, and fresh, everyday language are qualities I admire and aspire to as a writer. I especially love his short poems, which I call "snapshot poems," in which, with a few deft strokes, Williams captures a luminous moment that reveals a certain character, feeling, or social situation. One of my favorites, "Young Woman at a Window," reminds me of those line drawings I had to do in my studio art class in college, looking only at my subject, never lifting the pencil from the sketching pad:

> She sits with
> tears on
>
> her cheek
> her cheek on
>
> her hand
> the child
>
> in her lap
> his nose
>
> pressed
> to the glass

Another favorite seems, at first glance, a merely humorous glimpse at a young woman who has run out for a moment on an errand. (Why else

1

would she be bareheaded and still wearing her apron?) But the title charges the poem with political significance:

Proletarian Portrait

A big young bareheaded woman
in an apron

Her hair slicked back standing
on the street

One stockinged foot toeing
the sidewalk

Her shoe in her hand. Looking
intently into it

She pulls out the paper insole
to find the nail

That has been hurting her

What so amazes me about these poems is their utter simplicity, their economy of shape, and the way they capture the magic of the commonplace. They show how form can become transparent, ordering but not diminishing the chaotic fullness of experience, without frills or embellishments. In fact, every time I read one of Williams's simple little poems I am reminded of visiting my first museum with my father when we were newly arrived in this country. We stood in front of an abstract canvas filled with lines and dots and squares of color, and my father shook his head and said, "That's art?! I can do that!"

In fact, these qualities are not so easy to achieve. But they are precisely the qualities I like to promote in the work of my young student writers, which is why I often use Williams's poems as models in my writing workshops. Anyone who started teaching poetry workshops back in the 1970s remembers Kenneth Koch's wonderful book about teaching great poetry to children, *Rose, Where Did You Get That Red?* Koch discovered that even very young children found Williams's poems extremely appealing. In one exercise, Koch asked his students to write apology poems about things they were secretly glad they had done. Williams's poem, "This Is Just to Say," was the model:

This Is Just to Say

I have eaten
the plums
that were in
the icebox

and which
you were probably
saving
for breakfast

Forgive me
they were delicious
so sweet
and so cold

Like Koch, I've found that my college students, though older, also respond warmly to Williams's poems. The deceptively simple poems convince even my most reluctant beginning poets that they can "do" poetry. In fact, my students' reaction to Williams's poems is much like as my father's reaction to Joan Miró's abstact paintings: "Hell, I can do that."

So, I always start the poetry segment of the writing workshop—at Middlebury College our beginning workshops are dual genre—with one of Williams's snapshot poems, "Young Woman at a Window" or "Proletarian Portrait" or "This Is Just to Say." I go over all the wonderful qualities in them: their simple language; concrete images and telling details; form that illuminates content; line breaks that "meter" and "notate" the speaking voice, so that it becomes charged, as it does when we speak with feeling. Then, I send my students home with their first assignment: using Williams's poem as a model, take a snapshot of a person in a moment that reveals that person.

Surprisingly, the poems the students turn in are often full of abstractions, of explanations of the images presented, of adjectives that cloud the view by touching up the subjects, much like old-time photographers used to touch up daguerreotypes, so that even horse-faced great-aunts look like beauties. Any writing teacher will know what I mean.

My students think they are doing precisely what I asked them to do. They believe their poems are similar to the Williams poems. These are smart, ambitious, talented young people, but by the time I get them in college, they have acquired bad writing habits, which they don't even know they have. The root of these bad habits is that my students have started to write like English majors. They have forgotten how to simply look at something. Instead, they immediately begin to interpret, to find "hidden meanings," to analyze, and then to present the finished products of their exquisite lit-crit skills to me, their teacher.

Listen, I say to them, you're writing poetry like critics. You have to write poetry like poets. I quote what Flannery O'Connor said about fiction writing, which holds true for poetry writing as well: "There's a certain grain of stupidity that the writer of fiction can hardly do without, and this is the quality of having to stare, of not getting to the point at once." But my students want to get their points across—after all, that is what they have been taught to do in their other English classes.

One way I discovered to help my students break free is to show them what a Williams poem might have looked like if *he* had followed *their* example—explaining, abstracting, analyzing, philosophizing, etc. Of course, I don't say this straight out or I would put my sensitive and talented young students on the defensive. And what I am trying to do by using Williams's work is to encourage my students to feel a sense of playfulness and pleasure in seeing and recording in fresh, precise language the everyday world around them (a red wheelbarrow, the broken pieces of a green bottle, a locust tree in flower).

Soon after their first assignments come in, I bring in two versions of a Williams poem—or, I should say, I bring in a poem by Williams as well as my own ticket to hell. My ticket to hell is a rewrite of a Williams poem, say, "To a Poor Old Woman," in which I commit all the sins that I have spotted in my students' snapshot poems. I read these two poems and ask my students to tell me which one they think is the final draft of a Williams poem, and which one might be his "earlier draft."

Poverty

I saw a poor old lady,
and I felt so sorry for her:
poverty is such a disgrace.

But there are a few
moments of joy
even in the worst lives
when hunger is truly
satisfied,

even if it's only by a little
piece
of fruit. The poor many
times
appreciate it more than we
do.

And so a cheap little plum
can seem like a treasure.
I saw a poor old lady

eating a tiny fruit
with such relish
that you could tell that

for a moment she
wouldn't
for all the world give
away
her little fruit.

Oh, she felt like a queen
with a whole kingdom in
her hand!
And it was just a cheap
old plum.

To a Poor Old Woman

munching a plum on
the street a paper bag
of them in her hand

They taste good to her
They taste good
to her. They taste
good to her

You can see it by
the way she gives herself
to the one half
sucked out in her hand

Comforted
a solace of ripe plums
seeming to fill the air
They taste good to her

I would be exaggerating, of course, if I told you that all my students pick the second poem as the authentic or final draft of the Williams poem. One time a student mystified me by saying that she thought the two poems "go great together." But overall, I would say that the majority of my students know which one is the better poem. Even the holdouts are usually convinced as the discussion proceeds.

Once we have some consensus, I go line by line over both versions, asking my students why we are getting a clearer picture in the true Williams poem.

To start, I have them look closely at my miswrite. Even the title concludes for the reader what he or she is to make of the image: poverty. We haven't even entered the poem, and we already have the interpretation. Williams's poem, however, not only gives us an image, but uses the title as both a dedication of the poem and as the first line. Talk about economy of form! Less is more. We are pulled right into the picture, as greedy to read the next line as the old woman is greedy to devour the plum in her hand.

The first stanza of my miswrite gives us a picture of the poor, old lady, but by introducing herself into the picture, the poet is already distracting us from what should be the poem's focus, "*I saw* a poor old lady." This is a good place to bring up the issue of word choice, the tiny but important implications of using one word instead of another. Dickinson once said that there are no approximate words in a poem: we must have just the right one. Which is the right one in this instance? What picture does *old lady* evoke as opposed to *old woman*? What is the difference between these two kinds of senior citizens? (And what about using the words *senior citizen*?!) Which of these two kinds of senior citizens is sweet and talcumed, belonging to polite society, with a seasonal corsage on her winter coat, who would probably eat her plum with a knife and fork? Which of these two would be more likely to eat a plum as if—well, as if she were having sex—*giving herself* to the one half sucked out in her hand? There is something definitely alluring about Williams's woman, even if she is old and poor. In fact, she has inspired the poet to dedicate the poem to her. Traditionally, only beauties and lovely, languishing ladies rated that kind of literary attention.

Back to the miswrite: as soon as we get the picture in that first line, we are back to the writer's reaction and analysis of the image—for three more stanzas! "I felt so sorry for her . . . the poor many times appreciate it more than we do. . . ." The writer keeps blocking our view. Note, too, that the author of "Poverty" uses the past tense, a more removed, already-processed-by-memory tense, rather than the more immediate present tense of the real Williams poem. By the end of the first stanza of Williams's poem, we are munching away on those plums (and *munching* is a such a wonderful, munching verb). Meanwhile, in the miswrite, we are sitting in the high cathedral of literature, falling asleep, listening to a dull sermon about poverty being such a disgrace.

In the second stanza of the original Williams poem, we come upon those delightful, cadenced repetitions that convey the pleasure of eating that plum:

1—2—3
They taste good to her

1—2
They taste good

3—1
to her. They taste

2—3
good to her

Ever watch a little girl eating something she likes? She hums, rocks herself from side to side with each measured bite. Here the form mirrors that rhythmic, creaturely pleasure. Williams plays with those line breaks so that the three key words in the poem (*taste, good, her*) find their way to the emphatic position at the end of the line, as if the form were savoring and lingering over each of the words that—like the taste of those plums—sound so good to the reader's ears.

But Williams knows he can't just keep telling you that the plums taste good to her. Even after he's shown you—with the repetitions and line breaks—how they taste good to her, he's going to let you see for yourself: "You can see it by / the way *she gives herself* / to the one half / *sucked out* in her hand." The hunger and desire come out in the word choices—as shown in the phrases I've italicized. At the end of the poem we get that last, wonderful repetition of the earlier "refrain": "They taste good to her." By now we are in total agreement with Williams, because we have shared an intimate moment with this woman and tasted those plums *with* her.

The miswrite, meanwhile, labors away at making its point. We don't really know what fruit the old lady is eating, only that it is "tiny." We don't see how she eats this tiny fruit. We are told, not shown, that the old lady wouldn't give the whole world away for that plum. The claim is exaggerated and unearned. We start to mistrust the author.

But the ghost poet of this poem initially set out with the best intentions. In fact, I would agree with her politics. Poverty is such a disgrace; even a street person deserves a good meal, etc. The problem is that the author is giving her readers an analyzed portrait of poverty rather than presenting us with the thing itself—the thing that will, as the eleventh-century Chinese poet Wei T'ai promised, "convey the feeling":

> Poetry presents the thing in order to convey the feeling. It should be precise about the thing and reticent about the feeling. For as soon as the mind responds and connects with the thing, the feeling shows in the words. This is how poetry enters deeply into us.[1]

Mark Twain once told a young playwright who had written a scene in which one character comes on stage to tell another character that their old neighbor lady is upset and screaming: "Don't tell me the old lady screamed. Bring her on and let her scream!"

There are many more contrasts to be made between the two poems: between the use of mechanical and effective line breaks; "visible" and efficient—and, therefore, "invisible"—form; abstract and concrete language; and so on. Line by line, my students register these infinitesimal differences that add up to two such different poems. In this way, they experience the process by which a good poem achieves its results. Hopefully, my students also see where it is that their own snapshots went astray from the model they meant to emulate.

I am not saying that we reach a Helen Keller moment of illumination in which my students see that *water* means water. But I have found that these miswrites of Williams often show my students—rather than *tell* them—what is wrong with certain bad writing habits. And the best part of it is that no one needs to feel defensive because his or her workshop poem has been "torn apart" to prove a point. And hey, if Williams can write a bad poem, there's hope for all of us!

Well. . . . At this point in the workshop, I have to confess that I, not Williams, am the author of the bad poem. After all, I don't want to do double time in hell—as a liar as well as a plagiarist. For the next workshop, I print up this poem along with the others:

This Is Just to Say

I have rewritten
your poems
which were already
delicious

sweet and cold
as ripe plums
and eye-catching
like the broken

pieces of
a green bottle.
Sorry . . . it was
for a good cause,

poetry.

After the miswrite exercise, one of my students went back and revised her earlier poem. Her subtle revisions did make a difference. Here is her original poem:

In the Dining Room, Late at Night

Stealing down the hall in her pajamas,
She hears a sound,
A breath, muffled,
From the dark dining room.

He sits at the table.
His head is bowed,
So that he seems
As if he were
A paper cut-out
Against the white draperies.

His glasses, steamed with grief
And frustration,
Sit foreign
Unseeing,
On the table before him.

To make sure—
A little white-flanneled figure of comfort
Lays a childish hand on his
Shaking shoulders
While her father continues to cry.

Here is her revision:

In the Dining Room, Late at Night

Stealing down the hall in her pajamas
she hears
a muffled breath
coming from the
black dining room.

Sitting at the table,
head bowed,
he is a paper cut-out
against the white draperies.

His glasses sit foreign,
unseeing,
on the table before him.

She goes to him
on cold bare feet
and lays her hand
on her father's
solid shoulders
that shake
while he cries.

—*Mary Fitzpatrick, undergraduate, University of Illinois*

Note

1. Quoted in David Huddle, *The Writing Habit* (Hanover, N.H.: Univ. Press of New England, 1991), p. 16.

Kenneth Koch

Poems Inspiring Poems
Teaching William Carlos Williams in the Sixth Grade

This Is Just to Say

I have eaten
the plums
that were in
the icebox

and which
you were probably
saving
for breakfast

Forgive me
they were delicious
so sweet
and so cold

The Locust Tree in Flower

Among
of
green

stiff
old
bright

broken
branch
come

white
sweet
May

again

Between Walls

the back wings
of the

hospital where
nothing

will grow lie
cinders

in which shine
the broken

pieces of a green
bottle

I taught these three poems in one sixth grade class, having the children write poems with each. The lesson moved along quickly and turned out to be a very rich and interesting one. It was the children who set the pace for it; I had come to class thinking I would have time to teach one, or at the most two of the poems. But they were excited by them all and seemed in a mood to write one poem after another. The Williams poems are, in fact, simple and, if presented in the right way, extremely appealing to children. Once they knew what a poem was about, they wanted to write. The hour was busy but it didn't seem rushed. The very fact that they wrote so many poems (some children wrote six or seven) in one hour seemed to add to their feeling of inspiration and freedom and to put them in a fairly wild and receptive creative mood. Themes and techniques were carried over from one poem to the next, and the excitement of having written one poem became a creative excitement for writing the next one.

I began by giving everyone the three poems to read, then talked about them a little. One reason I'd decided to teach them was to give my students an example of a poet who wrote in ordinary language about ordinary things, so I talked about that. Also, I asked them if they liked the short lines, and if they liked the poem being so small and about just one thing. In fact, they did—the shortness and simplicity of the poems gave them the special pleasure of being able to think of an entire poem at once—a poem that could be written quickly, a single statement with only one or two words in a line.

I began with "This Is Just to Say," which has a theme children find irresistible, and which I used for the poetry idea: apologizing for something you're really secretly glad you did. Apologizing was a new note in their poetry and they enjoyed it; they enjoyed, too, asserting the importance of their secret pleasure against the world of adult regulations. They apologized for, and were pleased about, breaking things, taking things, forgetting and neglecting things, eating things, hitting people, and looking at things.

After they had finished these poems, I collected them and read a few aloud. Then I went on to "The Locust Tree in Flower," concentrating in that poem on its form: the use of one-word lines, and the disjointedness—the poem isn't a sentence but a series of individual words used somewhat like brushstrokes in a painting: each word adds something to what one sees, but it's not till near the end that one knows what the whole picture is. To make sure the children understood how this worked, I had them do a class collaboration. I stood at the blackboard and wrote down the words they called out to me to be lines for the poem. There was a sort of informal vote on each word (line). If we didn't like it, I asked for other suggestions. The children were delighted with this activity, and wanted to go on to another class poem, but I asked them to write poems of their own. The poetry idea was to write a poem about something you see, with one word in every line. I asked the children to try not to make the poem a sentence but to make it jagged like "The Locust Tree in Flower."

Excited by the collaboration and the idea of one word per line, the children wrote quickly and well. Some poems had a vividness of a kind I hadn't seen in even their best Comparison Poems—Andrew's about Coke, for example; Guy's about a dandelion; Jorge's about a wheel; and Vivien's "Thunder in Sky," which used Williams's techniques on a somewhat more complex kind of subject matter. The one-word-at-a-time brushstroke technique freed them from the burden of complete sentences and helped them to see and write about things sharply and freshly.

After collecting and reading a few of these poems, I asked the children if they felt up to another one. They said yes, so we did "Between Walls." What I concentrated on here was the un-beautifulness of the broken glass bottle and how Williams thinks it is beautiful anyway. I had chosen this poem because even more clearly than the other two it could point the children away from "highly poetical" things, like palaces and snowcapped mountains, as the only proper ones to write poetry about. It could help them to look for what was beautiful to them in the things they really saw. The poetry idea was, "Write a poem about something not supposed to be beautiful but which you really secretly think is, the way Williams thinks the glass behind the hospital is beautiful." I asked them for examples, to be sure they were thinking about really plain things. They wrote about the beauty of tin cans, charcoal, glass, a shining broken vase, garbage, a paper cup torn into little pieces.

There were various carry-overs from one poem to another—one-word-a-line apologies, for example, and the use of the "Locust Tree" brushstroke technique in the ugly-beautiful poems, such as Rafael's about the can. All three Williams poems carry a sense of the brightness and beauty of plain things and of a plain way of talking about them. They reinforce each other, and the children got a lot, I think, from having them all together. One thing was a new feeling for what a line of poetry was and for going from one line to another without completing a statement.

These sixth grade students had been enthusiastically writing poetry for several years, and so felt free about writing and had a great many ideas. Not every group of students will be able to work that hard at poetry for an hour. A good class could be made out of any one or two of these poems.

Short poems have an obvious appeal for children and suggest easy and pleasant things for them to write. Of those I know, I think these and a few others by Williams are among the best to teach them. Haiku are widely used as a poetry model for children. If haiku are used, I'd suggest ignoring their restrictive syllable count and de-emphasizing their often remote subject matter: snowy slopes, delicate bamboo shoots, shimmering pools, and other things most schoolchildren don't get to see much of. Williams's short poems give children the haiku-like pleasure of short lines without the haiku-like restrictions, and they suggest as subjects things that are a regular part of their lives.

1. THIS IS JUST TO SAY

Dear Dog
Please
for

give
me
for
eating
your
dog
biscuit.

    —*Lorraine Fedison*

Dear Biscuit

I'm
so
sorry
for
taking
you
away
from
your
friend
the
Dog.

    —*Mayra Morales*

Sorry but It Was Beautiful

Sorry I took your money and burned it but it looked
    like the world falling apart when it crackled and
    burned.
So I think it was worth it after all you can't see the
    world fall apart every day.

    —*Andrew Vecchione*

Sorry and Good

I
Dropped
a
glass
Nice
and

Sparkling
color
but
sorry
I
am
and
Glad
I
am
too.

 —*Vilma Mejias*

Dear Cat

Please
for
give
me
for
watching
your
eyes
gleam
in
the
night.

 —*Lorraine Fedison*

This Is Just to Say

That the dog
tore your
shoes in
to little pieces
and I let him
do it. It was quite amusing.

 —*Vivien Tuft*

The Red Flag

I
am
sorry
I
have
eaten
a
red
a
blue
a
white?
flag
but
I
ate
cause
I
was
hungry.

—*Miklos Lengyel*

I Just Want to Say

I have eaten
The flowers
That were
On your head
Which you
Were probably
Saving for
A funeral
Please forgive
Me.
I liked to say
You looked great
In a coffin
I'll bury you
For what I did
Please forgive me

—*Rafael Camacho*

2. THE LOCUST TREE IN FLOWER

Rose
Among
its
ground
lies
petals
red
small
thorns
green
   —*Class Collaboration*

Thunder in Sky
Among
   morning
      sky
         myself
      sees
         pink
         white

blue
         cotton
         clouds
      thunder
         rain
            me.

   —*Vivien Tuft*

The Colored Color
I
saw
a
pink
orange
purple
black

green
colored
color

    —Lorraine Fedison

The Bird

sky
clouds
wings
gray
up
down
flap
flip

    —Marion Mackles

Among
the
tree
is
thee
in
love
with
a
man
with
the
face
of
a
dog.

    —Ileana Mesen

Dandelion

around
the
body
lies
fur

which
is
on
top
of
a
stem
which
is
all
yellow.

    —Guy Peters

Fear

I
feared
my
Shadow
But
It
was
nice
to
see
myself
in
fear.

    —Vilma Mejias

Coke

Among
water
lies
sun
purple
green
red
coke
splatters
in
water

like
petals
on
roses
floating
in
the
sun
set
of
the
world

   —Andrew Vecchione

Greenbird

Among
its
feet
lie
feathers
green
pointed
beak
chirps
a
song
on
the
willow tree
it
is
a
greenbird

   —Lisa Smalley

The Rolling Wheel

Among
the
cement
wheels
chains

Ride
with
slowness
and
turns

    —Jorge Robles

3. BETWEEN WALLS

The Deserted Road

There was a very old deserted road
I took a walk on it,
And all of a sudden I saw the most beautiful thing
That I had ever seen on this road.
A paper cup torn into little pieces.

    —Vivien Tuft

The Charcoal

Inside the base
ment

where there
is no beauty

lies a piece
of crumbled
up black

dark charcoal
shining from the

flaming fire
and soon to
join the fire

    —Rafael Camacho

The Dirty Can

Along
the
street

rolls
an
old
crumbled
shining
with
beauty
a
can

   —Rafael Camacho

The ticking of the clock
Came from the wall above
Filled with bricks and wood.
The sound of a broken dish filled the air.

   —Jeannie Turner

Nothing Made to Something

The garbage I saw was like millions of crayon marks
    on paper.
It looks like the fire crackers of the world being shot
    off,
But the best thing was it looked like itself—ugly, but
    nice in a way.

   —Andrew Vecchione

It
was
just
a
big
fat
old
hunk
junk
but
I
like
it
cause

he
was
my
brother

    —Jorge Robles

Behind the door
    there is a person
    with eyes of
    blue that shine
    like a mirror
    when it's clean
Behind the door
    there is a
    girl who is
    I'd better
    not tell you.

    —Ileana Mesen

On the Other Side of the Window

On the other
Side of the
Window in
School lies
The playground
And how I long
To be on the
Other side
Of the
Window

    —Tommy Kennedy

Mary Edwards Wertsch

Finding the Magic in the Ordinary and Everyday

I teach poetry writing to inner-city St. Louis elementary school students who have had little prior exposure to the subject. Usually I work with the same class once a week for a whole semester. The first meeting with them is crucial for setting the right tone and establishing certain points I will return to again and again throughout the semester.

The two main points I want to drive home during that first lesson are that playing with language is rewarding for everyone—not just kids with track records of academic success—and that when it comes to finding something to write about, our own lives provide the best material. I've tried a variety of ways to do this, but perhaps the most effective is to teach a lesson on William Carlos Williams.

The first time I meet with a class, I tell them how much I love poetry and poetry writing, and how glad I am to be able to share this with them. I tell them that I feel one of the best ways to introduce other people to this subject I love so much is to show them a poem I really like, explore that poem with them, and then use it as a model for our own writing that day.

"Don't worry about that last part," I inteject. "By the time we start to write, you'll know exactly what you're supposed to do, and I will have read you examples of what other kids your age have written when they did this same exercise. Also, you don't have to worry about spelling. Spelling is something we can take care of together later. What we're doing here is about having fun with language—what I call 'playing the poetry game.' I'll tell you more as we go along."

Then I write W-I-L-L-I-A-M C-A-R-L-O-S W-I-L-L-I-A-M-S on the board, in very large letters. Students often marvel at the similarity of his first and last names. Then we look at the middle name. I ask them to guess what language a person named Carlos might speak. Then I tell them that Williams's mother came from Puerto Rico, and that he knew the Spanish language and even used Spanish words in the middle of a poem written in English.

I write the dates of his birth and death on the board (1883–1963), then do subtraction to show how old he was when he died. Then I proceed with his biography.

"William Carlos Williams was born and raised in Rutherford, New Jersey, and from childhood he loved words and books and poems. He tried writing poems himself, and he became quite good at it. William Carlos Williams figured out he wanted to be a poet. By this time he was in college, around 1905. He had friends who were planning to be poets, too.

"Many poets of that time, thought that you couldn't be a serious poet and remain in the United States. They actually thought that you had to go all the way across the Atlantic Ocean and live in England or France or Italy, and write about very grand subjects like war and romance. But William Carlos Williams saw things differently. Why turn your back on the things and the people you know best? You can write poems anywhere, and about anything! He proved that you can make beautiful, powerful poems about ordinary, everyday things.

"There was another thing Williams wanted to be besides a poet, and that was a medical doctor. He graduated from medical school and went back to his home town, where he practiced medicine for forty years and delivered 2,000 babies! He was very dedicated to being a doctor and helping people. But he was just as dedicated to being a poet. It would often happen that he would get an idea for a poem while walking down the halls of the hospital or while he was treating his patients. Every writer knows that when you get a good idea, you have to write it down fast! So he'd tear a page off of his prescription pad, jot down the idea on it, and stick it in his pocket. At night, when he was back at home again, he'd empty out his pockets and turn the notes into poems.

"Dr. Williams wrote many books of poetry. He began receiving attention for his fine work and the way it inspired other poets. By the end of his life he had won most of the big prizes poets can win. He proved that you can write excellent poems about ordinary, everyday things."

Next I tell the kids I'm going to prove his point about ordinary, everyday things. On the blackboard I write out one of his short poems about the everyday, among which are "Complete Destruction," about the burial of a cat; "Mujer," about a black Persian cat; "Silence," about autumn leaves and a bird; or "Nantucket" describing a hotel room in summertime. Usually I choose "The Red Wheelbarrow."

As I write it on the board, I explain that it's important to copy the poem accurately, with its short lines.

We talk about the meaning of the words—*glazed*, for instance. (Doughnut!) I ask them if they have ever noticed how shiny and colorful cars are after a rainstorm. Then we look at the lines "so much depends / upon."

"Now, we could spend a happy half-hour talking about what he might mean by that," I say. "And I want you to know that you, the reader, always get to decide what the poem means to you. There is no single right meaning for a poem. You get to be the boss!

"But for me what he's saying here is that so much depends upon *noticing* that wheelbarrow. That's the part he did himself. I feel sure other people had walked right by that bright red wheelbarrow and not paid attention to it. But he did, and that made all the difference.

"The same thing can be true for you and me and everyone else, too. If you take the time to open your eyes and really notice what's around you, it becomes special and powerful and almost magical. Your heart opens up to the special message of an object, a scene, an everyday event. Suddenly it—and you—are lifted up out of the ordinary.

"I want you to think of something you have noticed in your home, your neighborhood, or your school. Something ordinary and everyday— but you noticed it, you remembered it, and now you're going to make me notice it too, through your words.

"We're going to follow the model of William Carlos Williams's poem—simple words, short lines, a picture drawn in words. But instead of starting off with 'so much depends upon,' let's start with a question: 'Have you seen?' And that's going to be the last line of your poem, too. Why repeat it? Because that's a way of making your readers know that you think it's really important for them to notice this, as though you're taking them by the collar and shaking them. Have you *noticed* this? Have you really *noticed* this thing I'm talking about? Don't you know how important it is to really notice what's around you?

"Now, here are my rules. First, no rhyming. William Carlos Williams didn't rhyme his poem, and I don't want you to, either. Not today.

"Second, no making anything up; another time we will do that. But today I want you to write about something you really did see.

"And third, remember to use describing words to make a sharp picture. When you hand me a poem you've written, it's as though you just put a little television set down in front of me. When I start to read your poem, the TV set clicks on. But the picture is very fuzzy. The more describing words you use, the sharper that picture comes in—until finally I have the same picture in my head that you had in *yours*. And *that's* what playing the poetry game is all about.

"What kinds of things can you think of to write about? Here are some examples by other kids."

Have you seen?
The bright red
apple sitting
in the tree
way out of reach
Have you seen?

   —Dareaux Dyson, fifth grade

Have you seen?
A crayfish in water
not knowing
how to swim
and it fears
for its life
and doesn't know
what to do
Have you seen?

   —Courtnie McKinney, fifth grade

A young child
with shackles
on his wrist
getting put into
a car
with bright lights
and sirens
Have you seen?

   —Jeremy Greene, fifth grade

Have you seen?
My dead fish

in the top
of the pot
floating around
in circles
Have you seen?

  —*David Johnson, second grade*

Have you seen?
A white
police truck
in the black
street
Have you seen?

  —*Terrelle, second grade*

Have you seen?
A book without pages
like a person
that needs something.
Have you seen?

  —*Sadé Carter, fourth grade*

Have you seen?
A dog's eyes
lighting up
like black and green
jewels
Have you seen?

  —*John Green, third grade*

Have you seen?
The burned
up house
when the weather
is bad—
the old woman
looks out

the window.
Have you seen?

> — *Herbert Gold, fifth grade*

Have you seen?
A white rope
on the floor in
the living room
stretched out
like a pencil
ready
for Double Dutch

> —*Salena, second grade*

Have you seen?
The moon so bright
in the dark blue sky
and the sun so bright
in the light blue sky
and a little boy
looking up at it
have you seen?

> —*Ronald Hampton, third grade*

Have you seen?
The rain looks
like little people
diving into a river
Have you seen?

> —*Shaun Brown, third grade*

Have you seen?
The sun shining
on a motionless
lake
Have you seen?

> —*Calvin Hailey, fifth grade*

Have you seen?
The shining Arch
a pile
of silver bricks
gleaming, blind
Have you seen?

    —Sharaela Riggens, fifth grade

Sometimes students take the assignment in new directions:

Have you heard?
The wind sounding
like a classical song,
you twirling in its warmth,
you prancing to its beat
Have you heard?

    —Sharaela Riggens, fifth grade

Have you heard?
The wind swish
—and swash
all over the city
the car horns honking
and people
yelling and screaming
sirens wailing
Have you heard?

    —LaShawn Glass, fifth grade

Using the repeated question gives students a framing device, but it's possible with some groups to delete the last line—and even the first—in revision.

Often in connection with this lesson I tell my students about Martin, a third grader. The first time I entered his classroom, I saw him seated at a desk that was set apart from everyone else's.

The teacher told me, "You don't have to worry about Martin. He won't be able to do what you're asking. You just teach the other kids and forget about him."

But Martin listened to the lesson and he understood right away that to play the poetry game, you don't have to get good grades in other subjects. It's about imagination and a willingness to make something happen with words, tell something in a new way. The poems Martin wrote—which he sometimes made up out loud while I squatted next to him and wrote them down—were wonderful. When I read them to his class and the other classes in the school, the kids burst into applause.

Below is a "have you seen" poem by Martin. Children like it because it is intriguing, like the start of a short story:

> Have you seen?
> Dead flowers—
> orange, pink,
> green and yellow—
> in some bushes,
> like somebody
> was mad.
> Have you seen?

I have noticed that after hearing about Martin, some of the students at the bottom of the class or with reputations for nonparticipation get right down to work, producing several poems, often strong ones. That's one of the reasons I love teaching this particular lesson. It reassures students that they have plenty of things they can write about, and that their own perceptions are as valid as anyone's. Just as Williams found value in the everyday, the students find value in themselves.

Peggy Garrison

Pushing the Red Wheelbarrow
From Age Five to Sixty-five

Some of the most effective poems are those whose images seemingly took the poet by surprise, giving the poem veracity and freshness—that amazement, as Theodore Roethke said, of having "come to something without knowing why." A woman eating a plum, a white bed, a wet red wheelbarrow next to white chickens—Williams rediscovered common things in his poems and gave them special framing.

I wanted students to explore spontaneous ways of finding material for their poems by suppressing control over their subject matter and letting their unconscious minds do the work. Putting themselves in a heightened state of waiting, they could discover the poetic quality of everyday things. At the time, I was working at opposite ends of the student spectrum, teaching a K–2 poetry residency at a public school in Queens, N.Y., and an adult poetry workshop in continuing education in Manhattan, so I chose a poem I thought might work with both age groups: "The Red Wheelbarrow."

With the younger grades, I began by writing the poem and the poet's name on the board:

so much depends
upon

a red wheel
barrow

glazed with rain
water

beside the white
chickens

—*William Carlos Williams*

Then I read the poem aloud, and, because I feel it's important for students to view poets as human beings rather than remote deities, I showed them Williams's picture. I told them he was a doctor and that he came from New Jersey. I asked how many students had ever been to New Jersey. Then we examined the poem. I wanted to be sure students understood the meaning of the words *glazed* and *wheelbarrow* (some confused *barrow* with *barrel*). Next we talked about how live chickens and a red wheelbarrow (rather than a gray one full of concrete) suggested a rural or small-town setting rather than an urban one. Then because I felt the phrase "so much depends upon" might be misleading, I explained that it could have meanings other than that of children's being dependent on their parents or of people's being dependent on food; it could also mean "this is important" or "this is special." I urged the students to imagine themselves to be Williams, leaving a farmhouse, walking slowly to his car, when suddenly chickens and a wheelbarrow seemed to pop out in front of him and command, "Write about me!"

The idea of images "popping out" delighted them. I asked them to look around the classroom to see if anything popped out at them and seemed to demand that they write about it. With excitement the kindergartners dictated a list that I wrote on a big piece of oaktag. It included:

a big red apple
made of crunched-up paper

Mrs. Bush's
red and blue striped snake

that pink hippopotamus
with the green house on it

my painting of spaceships
shooting at each other

those four ghosts
on the wall

the flowers for
good behavior on
the blackboard

Equally enthusiastic, the first and second graders wrote their observations individually. Marybeth wrote:

The Pouches

people depend on these
colorful bags with dots
and patterns all magnificent
things on these carriers
all made of wool and glue

this is my magnificent
thing

   —Marybeth Vallejo

When I returned the following week, my classes continued their attentiveness to "pop-out" images, only this time, like Williams, we went outside. It was a lovely late-spring day and the students were thrilled to be taking this little field trip. Notepads and pencils ready, attention heightened, we walked around the school block, noticing things.

When we got back to the room, I gave the students five extra minutes to finish writing or make changes before we read aloud. The assignment had been simply to record images accurately. Though some students did closely follow the assignment, others surprised me by expanding their observations into poems.

Jolene wrote an ode:

The Pigeons

Oh pigeons oh pigeons
come to me oh pigeons
oh pigeons come to
me your feathers are
gray they brighten my
day your beaks
are orange and brown
they make my day
so round and then
the day is down oh
pigeons oh pigeons
come to me.

   —Jolene Klusko, second grade

The following piece is reminiscent of another Williams poem, "The Term," which is about a piece of paper that gets run over in the street:

As I walk around the school block
I see a black and blue rope
in the middle of the street
but then the poor rope
gets run over by two cars,
one a jeep and the other
a gray wagon. "OUCH THAT
MUST HURT."

> —*Jillian Tomm, second grade*

Julian's poem has a sense of urgency:

An ant jumped out at me
and said write about me
or I will bite you. OK I said.

> —*Julian Kowlczyk, first grade*

As does Patrick's poem:

I see two big blue portable bathrooms.
They look shiny from the sun.
They have no doorknobs
and no locks.

> —*Patrick Fan, first grade*

In just two class periods the students learned a lot from Williams. They let themselves be inspired by common images; they were sensitive to colors; and most of them wrote in everyday speech rather than in "poetic" language.

Since the red wheelbarrow exercise was so successful with such young students, I was eager to see how it would work with my adult class, a very literate group of seven (two were high school English teachers) ranging in age from forty to sixty-five. In addition to the wheelbarrow poem, I handed out copies of "Nantucket" and "10/22," two other Williams poems that also reflect intense observation of everyday things.

Nantucket

Flowers through the window
lavender and yellow

changed by white curtains—
Smell of cleanliness—

Sunshine of late afternoon—
On the glass tray

a glass pitcher, the tumbler
turned down, by which

a key is lying—And the
immaculate white bed

10/22

that brilliant field
of rainwet orange
blanketed

by the red grass
and oilgreen bayberry

the last yarrow
on the gutter
white by the sandy
rainwater

and a white birch
with yellow leaves
and few
and loosely hung

and a young dog
jumped out
of the old barrel

First a student read the poems aloud, then I asked what all three
poems seemed to have in common. One student was especially impressed
by the accurate language of the examples and by how Williams created
these poems by accumulating images. Another student noted the fresh
presentation of common things and the use of colors. Instead of asking
the students to discover images in the classroom, I asked them to bring
in next time a list of things that seemed to demand their attention. I was
hesitant about using "pop out," fearing they'd feel I was treating them
as children. I suggested they think of themselves as fishing, but instead
of catching the fish (images), they let the fish catch them.

When we met the following week, I saw that a few poems could be
pulled directly from their lists:

At orange noon
this day-lily
leans against
the railings of
an iron fence.

   —*Anita Feldman*

five mail boxes
leaning towards and away
under an old maple

   —*David Quintavalle*

But generally the adults were less spontaneous and less enthusiastic than the younger students. Some felt they had to force their observations to conclusions. One student refused to write a list. He said he couldn't see any point in waiting for images. Another said that Williams's poems were pretty but they had no purpose. She preferred poems with a message. When I invited the class outside to write, two students wanted to stay in the classroom and rework their lists. They said they were tired.

Such resistance discouraged me. I began to question whether the exercise was going to work with this group. The younger students had welcomed the process, but the adults seemed reluctant to believe that through this method of attentiveness a poem could emerge.

I think Williams challenged their concept of poetry. Some felt that poems had to have conflicts and messages. To call descriptions and juxtapositions of simple images "poems" seemed baffling to them. One student kept saying, "But what's the point?" In addition, my emphasis on *discovering* material meant giving up conscious control, to trust the unconscious rather than suppress it. For some this was scary.

Just when I was starting to think this lesson was a flop, poems influenced by Williams began to show up in the workshop pile. The K–2 students had sparked immediately; being part of a group energized them. The adults, on the other hand, were experiencing the assignment slowly and individually. One student later said she'd "needed time to be haunted."

The new poems were spare and very focused, with more emphasis on the accumulation of images than the poems by the younger students:

7/30

Now the light
is hitting
the side of my face;
the cat
has stretched
and is looking
at me—
her cat eyes
studying
my posture
waiting
to see when
I will
get up and
fetch her
dinner.

   —*Judith Hawk*

Whately

Along the road are bi- and trifurcated trees
with bark bleeding
and old trunks painted with mold
under a canopy of leaves.

Cars and trucks announce their
coming and passing,
departing at a lower pitch.

Small planes putter above;
crows call below.

A sign shines on silver saw blade:

"J & M Service
   IRE REPAIRS

JOHN & MINNIE PILVINNIS"
An arrow points down Pilvinnis Avenue
to 16A and 16B.

   —*Hal Drooker*

One student brought a poem to class after her vacation in Italy. She told us she'd rendered it from "Williams-type" notes.

Train Station

The sun cuts across the tracks
pigeons on the roof of *binario due.*
Taxi drivers heavy lidded
lounge against the cement posts.
A rattly rock-and-roll song Italian-style
flows from a radio.
In the provincial train station
the young policeman, a dandy,
gun slung low,
chats with a fellow with
dark chest exposed through barely buttoned shirt.
Orange, purple, black designs,
sunglasses with white rims:
they shoot the breeze.

People study the schedule—
man with heavy belly, pants hanging below,
broad-topped woman tapering to thin black shirt,
bare skin showing,
quick mini-skirt hung on hips,
wraps narrow arms around him and presses close.

The sound of gentle, hoarse voices—
breezes,
an announcement,
the train hums into the Portogruaro station.

—*Nina Drooker*

Another student said that one evening when he was making potato salad he suddenly felt that the enjoyment of life was distilled into preparing this one dish.

All I Want from Potato Salad

Peel and boil
the sting of scallions
oregano, cumin, a pepper sneeze
the comfort of vinegar mixing

with the spices
lifted to my face
by the warmth of the potatoes.
    —*David Quintavalle*

In looking over both groups' poems, I was struck by how similarly they reflected Williams's influence. Though each group assimilated the exercise differently, both groups wrote about everyday objects, were sensitive to the use of color, and created an intense sense of the present.

Discussing the lesson with the adults afterward helped me refine it. I described my presentation in the K–2 classes and read some of the younger students' poems. I told them how with the children I'd carefully focused on the concept of images popping out, but was afraid of insulting adults by using the "pop-out" approach. Further, I thought they'd be offended if I cajoled them all into writing together outside. They said they might have caught on faster if I'd treated them more like the children and in the future I shouldn't worry about doing that. In fact they felt that the spirit of this exercise, with its sense of spontaneity and discovery, fully allowed for such treatment.

Ron Padgett

Other Plums

Neglected Short Poems by William Carlos Williams

Two of William Carlos Williams's poems—"The Red Wheelbarrow" and "This Is Just to Say"—are so popular that they overshadow other little gems of his that are also good models for writing.

For use with younger students, I particularly recommend four such poems: "Stormy," "Poem" ("As the cat . . ."), "Good Night," and "The Hurricane," all of which are clear and delightful. Here is the first one:

Stormy

what name could
better
explode from
a sleeping pup
but this
leaping

to his feet
Stormy!
Stormy! Stormy!

This deceptively simple poem is made up of a question that turns into exclamations. Originating in the name of a dog, the poem erupts the way a sudden storm does. After passing out the poem and reading it aloud with your students, ask them to think of the name—preferably a colorful one—of a pet they've had, and then to think of a lot of things that the name reminds them of. Then have the students write short poems that end in the repeated exclamation of the name.

For example, take the name Snowball. It makes one think of winter, whiteness, outdoors, whizzing projectiles, etc. A student might write something like this:

Snowball

what in the
cold air

I see
my breath
in
as I roll
around
is that barking
flying
toward my
face Snowball!
Snowball! Snowball!

An overall device of the following Williams poem is the description of a downward motion:

Poem

As the cat
climbed over
the top of

the jamcloset
first the right
forefoot

carefully
then the hind
stepped down

into the pit of
the empty
flowerpot

This poem is made up of one sentence, a sentence that, like time-lapse photography, keeps us suspended, wondering what is happening, until we get to the end. But at the end nothing exciting or dramatic happens, and perhaps that is the point: what is interesting is what happens along the way to the end. After presenting Williams's poem to your students, ask them each to write a poem in which something descends slowly, slowly enough for the writer to describe the stages of descent, as in:

The drop
of
rain
ran

down the
window
glass
and merged
into another
drop
to form
a solid
streak
that
at the frame
stopped.

The third Williams poem, "Good Night," presents a type of experience everyone has had:

Good Night

In brilliant gas light
I turn the kitchen spigot
and watch the water plash
into the clean white sink.
On the grooved drain-board
to one side is
a glass filled with parsley—
crisped green.
    Waiting
for the water to freshen—
I glance at the spotless floor—:
a pair of rubber sandals
lie side by side
under the wall-table
all is in order for the night.

Waiting, with a glass in my hand
—three girls in crimson satin
pass close before me on
the murmurous background of
the crowded opera—
       it is
memory playing the clown—
three vague, meaningless girls
full of smells and
the rustling sound of
cloth rubbing on cloth and

little slippers on carpet—
high-school French
spoken in a loud voice!

Parsley in a glass,
still and shining,
brings me back. I take my drink
and yawn deliciously.
I am ready for bed.

This poems has three parts: 1) a description of the place the speaker is in; 2) a sudden memory or daydream of something apparently far away and unrelated to the present moment; 3) a return to the present, which now feels different. As with many of Williams's poems, this one is pleasing partly because of the clear details of the scene. To demonstrate this clarity for students, you could rephrase the poem, omitting the details, as in:

I went into the kitchen
and stood there
and thought about something else,
then remembered where I was.

A good assignment is to write a poem that describes a scene, wanders away, and comes back. The classroom is the obvious example of a place students mentally wander from and then come back to.

The fourth example poem from Williams is weird and either grouchy or amusing or both, and will cause enemies of the comma splice to grit their teeth:

The Hurricane

The tree lay down
on the garage roof
and stretched, You
have your heaven,
it said, go to it.

Although the idea here is simple—have a basically immobile, non-speaking object move and talk to us—this poem turns out to be rather mysterious, insofar as we can't tell whether the tree is wishing us well or ill. Have your students write a poem in which a thing tells them or us what to do. Make sure the students know that it's okay to "let go," allowing their speaking objects to say things that even the students don't understand.

•

The above poems could be used by writers of any age, but the ones that follow are more suitable for older writers, due to their content.

Danse Russe

If I when my wife is sleeping
and the baby and Kathleen
are sleeping
and the sun is a flame-white disc
in silken mists
above shining trees,—
if I in my north room
dance naked, grotesquely
before my mirror
waving my shirt round my head
and singing softly to myself:
"I am lonely, lonely.
I was born to be lonely,
I am best so!"
If I admire my arms, my face,
my shoulders, flanks, buttocks
against the yellow drawn shades,—

Who shall say I am not
the happy genius of my household?

This much-anthologized poem, whose title means "Russian Dance," consists of a series of three "if" clauses that culminate in a "who" question. Even if we don't know who Kathleen is, the content of the poem is clear. Students like the poem because it reminds them of their own experience, for who among them has never looked at himself or herself naked in a mirror, or never done anything silly or goofy? Students are interested to see a great poet—a doctor yet!—"exposing" himself in these two ways.

Notice that in the three conditional clauses, Williams allows himself plenty of room for description and monologue, thus building up a syntactic pressure that is then released by the "who" clause. Have your students read and discuss the poem, then write one of their own, using a series of "if" clauses that end with a "who" question. Allow or even encourage variations: for instance, there needn't be an "I" in the poem. Encourage the students to let themselves go, if not autobiographically, then at least artistically. After all, the spirit of this poem is free and wacky.

Another good poem for older students is "The Young Housewife":

The Young Housewife

At ten A.M. the young housewife
moves about in negligee behind
the wooden walls of her husband's house.
I pass solitary in my car.

Then again she comes to the curb
to call the ice-man, fish-man, and stands
shy, uncorseted, tucking in
stray ends of hair, and I compare her
to a fallen leaf.

The noiseless wheels of my car
rush with a crackling sound over
dried leaves as I bow and pass smiling.

On the surface this poem describes a brief, glancing encounter, but not far beneath the surface lies a discreet eroticism. The suggestive line break ("negligee behind"), the virtual X-ray vision of the speaker, the absence of a corset, the touching of hair—all these suggest that the speaker finds the scantily clad young woman quite attractive. But he makes no overture. Like him, most of us have been attracted to someone—either for a moment or over a long period—without saying a word about it. Normally we think of such unrequited attraction as negative, but this poem brings to light the pleasure of secret eroticism. For writing students, this poem, a good example of the show-don't-tell dictum, can serve as a model for other poems or for prose vignettes about unspoken attraction.

Yet another of Williams's poems describes a secret pleasure:

The Thinker

My wife's new pink slippers
have gay pompons.
There is not a spot or a stain

on their satin toes or their sides.
All night they lie together
under her bed's edge.
Shivering I catch sight of them
and smile, in the morning.
Later I watch them
descending the stair,
hurrying through the doors
and round the table,
moving stiffly
with a shake of their gay pompons!
And I talk to them
in my secret mind
out of pure happiness.

Because the private happiness the speaker feels in this poem is not necessarily erotic, you could probably use this poem with younger students. The beauty of this poem—in addition to its quietness and domesticity—lies in its focus on the slippers, a focus so intent that when they move about the house, it's as if they are doing it all by themselves.

Have your students read the poem and then write about a common object they really like, using specific details (when I was a child I loved the glistening chrome head of an Indian that ornamented the hood of our family's Pontiac). It might be a good idea to choose an object, as Williams does, that gets moved around.

In Williams's "Portrait of a Lady," the speaker begins to praise his beloved, but things quickly go haywire:

Portrait of a Lady

Your thighs are appletrees
whose blossoms touch the sky.
Which sky? The sky
where Watteau hung a lady's
slipper. Your knees
are a southern breeze—or
a gust of snow. Agh! what
sort of man was Fragonard?
—as if that answered
anything. Ah, yes—below
the knees, since the tune
drops that way, it is
one of those white summer days,

the tall grass of your ankles
flickers upon the shore—
Which shore?—
the sand clings to my lips—
Which shore?
Agh, petals maybe. How
should I know?
Which shore? Which shore?
I said petals from an appletree.

Some students might need to be told that Williams is debunking the flourishes of lofty metaphors, and that Watteau and Fragonard were French artists who did idyllic paintings of impossibly gorgeous young women, often on swings. When these minor difficulties have been disposed of, students are often delighted to see a poem in which the poet talks back to himself (or gets snippy with someone else) and uses expressions like *agh*.

Have your students write a highly "poetic" line or two about a very beautiful or idealized person or landscape, but then start to question their own images, the way Williams does. Point out that the dash comes in handy in a poem that is built on interruptions and changes of direction.

•

I recommend five other good but neglected short poems by Williams as models for students: "To a Chinese Woman" and "The Counter," for their use of repetitions; "For a Low Voice," for its inclusion of words such as *huh*, *ha*, and *ho*; and "Young Woman at a Window" (the second version) and "Proletarian Portrait," for the economy of their portraiture. But the ultimate pleasure of selecting good poems for your students lies in leafing through the two volumes of Williams's *Collected Poems* yourself, where you will no doubt discover other overlooked and useful delights.

Charles North

"January Morning," or What Will You Not Be Experiencing?

Early in his poetic career, Williams wrote a delightful little ode to, of all things, his own nose ("Smell!")[1] in which he calls his nose and himself "tactless asses," unable to stem their "indiscriminate, always unashamed" attraction to all things including the "rank" and "unlovely." "What," he exclaims, "will you not be smelling?" The poem ends: "Must you taste everything? Must you know everything? / Must you have a part in everything?"

The answer to these playful questions, not merely for his nose but for Williams the poet, is Yes! (including the exclamation point). It is as though he can't help noticing and being excited by his surroundings, especially those parts that others often overlook: the unappealing, the apparently trivial or commonplace, the unlovely. And like his great predecessor Walt Whitman, he has the rare ability to make the unpromising details of life striking and even beautiful. These qualities make Williams's poetry a wonderful model for student writers.

Williams's pleasure in his surroundings is nowhere more evident than in "January Morning," a "Suite" of notations having to do with what it is like to be alive on a winter morning in New Jersey in the vicinity of the Hudson River.

January Morning
Suite:

    I

I have discovered that most of
the beauties of travel are due to
the strange hours we keep to see them:

the domes of the Church of
the Paulist Fathers in Weehawken
against a smoky dawn—the heart stirred—

are beautiful as Saint Peters
approached after years of anticipation.

II

Though the operation was postponed
I saw the tall probationers
in their tan uniforms

hurrying to breakfast!

III

—and from basement entries
neatly coiffed, middle aged gentlemen
with orderly moustaches and
well-brushed coats

IV

—and the sun, dipping into the avenues
streaking the tops of
the irregular red houselets,

and
the gay shadows dropping and dropping.

V

—and a young horse with a green bed-quilt
on his withers shaking his head:
bared teeth and nozzle high in the air!

VI

—and a semicircle of dirt-colored men
about a fire bursting from an old
ash can,

VII

—and the worn,
blue car rails (like the sky!)
gleaming among the cobbles!

VIII

—and the rickety ferry-boat "Arden"!
What an object to be called "Arden"
among the great piers,—on the
ever new river!

"Put me a Touchstone
at the wheel, white gulls, and we'll
follow the ghost of the *Half Moon*
to the North West Passage—and through!
(at Albany!) for all that!"

IX

Exquisite brown waves—long
circlets of silver moving over you!
enough with crumbling ice crusts among you!
The sky has come down to you,
lighter than tiny bubbles, face to
face with you!
                His spirit is
a white gull with delicate pink feet
and a snowy breast for you to
hold to your lips delicately!

X

The young doctor is dancing with happiness
in the sparkling wind, alone
at the prow of the ferry! He notices
the curdy barnacles and broken ice crusts
left at the slip's base by the low tide
and thinks of summer and green
shell-crusted ledges among
                the emerald eel-grass!

XI

Who knows the Palisades as I do
knows the river breaks east from them
above the city—but they continue south
—under the sky—to bear a crest of
little peering houses that brighten
with dawn behind the moody
water-loving giants of Manhattan.

XII

Long yellow rushes bending
above the white snow patches;
purple and gold ribbon
of the distant wood:

what an angle
you make with each other as
you lie there in contemplation.

XIII

Work hard all your young days
and they'll find you too, some morning
staring up under
your chiffonier at its warped
bass-wood bottom and your soul—
out!
—among the little sparrows
behind the shutter.

XIV

—and the flapping flags are at
half mast for the dead admiral.

XV

All this—
            was for you, old woman.
I wanted to write a poem
that you would understand.
For what good is it to me
if you can't understand it?
            But you got to try hard—
But—
      Well, you know how
the young girls run giggling
on Park Avenue after dark
when they ought to be home in bed?
Well,
that's the way it is with me somehow.[2]

The poem's fifteen sections come in no apparent order and are "unparallel," i.e., varied in content, tone, length, shape, rhetorical strategy, etc. What is immediately striking is how vividly and exuberantly Williams records what he notices. Williams's animated (and animating) sense of things is infectious and inspiring, as is his clear joy in being alive.

What might be called the democracy of his approach—a great variety of things treated with equal respect, emphasis, and enthusiasm—is displayed in the way Williams writes as much as in what he writes about.

He is determined to avoid Poetry with a capital P. The language he uses is colloquial and conversational and includes frequent exclamations, interruptions, afterthoughts that give the impression of someone speaking off the cuff, and words that strike some readers as "nonpoetic." Rather than formal devices such as regular stanzas, he prefers casual, even fragmentary notation: *this*, he seems to be saying, is *poetry* as much as anything else is. Even the length and shape of his enjambed lines, a number of which end with "little" words (*of, to, the, as*) add to this air of quick notation.

What Williams does in "January Morning" is, in effect, to follow his nose from one perception, feeling, idea, or association to another. At one point he is struck by "middle aged gentlemen / with orderly moustaches," then by the sun on the roofs of little houses, then by a horse rearing. In section VIII, the name of the ferry he is on provokes a miniature cadenza of associations: from "Arden" to *As You Like It* to Henrik Hudson and the Northwest Passage. One thing follows another not in a logical sense, but rather in the order it appears in the poet's awareness.

•

"January Morning" is one of my favorite Williams poems, and I have had success using it in college poetry-writing classes. It is essentially a list poem wherein each section is free to take on whatever characteristics the writer chooses. That freedom is inspiring to many students. They can choose almost anything as a springboard—a season, a place, an idea, a feeling, a name, an activity, even a conventional topic—and then follow their noses without predetermining any aspect of the individual sections. Nor need the final product resemble "January Morning." The important thing is to set out to write freely, with the permission Williams's poetry grants us to try new ways and to be honest rather than censor or tailor our feelings to some socially acceptable notion of what is fitting.

One method that often helps is to have students draft twenty sections, and then choose the best fifteen (or ten or five). Or they can simply brainstorm at first, with no thought about sections. This type of poem can also be thought of as Theme and Variations; but it is important to establish that the "theme" can be as firm or as flimsy as the writer likes. That is to say, it's perfectly all right for the nominal subject to be just that, an "excuse" for writing a poem that will find its own way thereafter. I have even suggested to some students, after discussing "January Morning" with them in some detail, that they begin with a title, and then purposely disregard the title in writing the poem. Sometimes Williams's exuberance and concreteness carry over into their poems even so, and the superficial discrepancy between the poem's title and body adds an intriguing dimension.

As a poet myself, I find a great many things about "January Morning" inspiring. Williams's way of writing as though he is right in the middle of what he writes about—rather than scribbling on a prescription pad at midnight after a sixteen-hour day as a physician, as was often the case—gives his poems an extraordinary immediacy. His stops and restarts and qualifications, as in the final section of the poem—which is also a playful but at bottom serious comment on his poetry in general—give the impression that he discovers what to write in the process of writing. His frequent use of a simple "and" to begin a section propels his poem forward. Students who follow their noses in this fashion often find themselves pleasantly surprised by what they come up with. The surprise is part of the excitement in writing poetry, as well as what makes many of the best traditional and contemporary poems exciting for readers. Of course Williams's poetic effects are not as easy to come by as he makes it seem; making it seem so is his gift. It is in fact rare for a writer to be so attentive to surroundings as well as to inner states, and to render both so vividly. What Williams says to the woman in the final section is equally important for student writers: "You got to try hard." But trying hard doesn't necessarily mean laboring over lines or individual words; especially for beginning poets, that approach to poetry can kill off all enthusiasm. Trying hard can mean trying to be as free and inclusive and honest as Williams is. What should be made clear to students is that regardless of the model, the composition of their poems is in every respect up to them, the goal being to produce writing that reflects at least some of the qualities of Williams's poem.

There are many other ways to present "January Morning" as a model, such as by focusing on its "dailiness" and general down-to-earthness. Also noteworthy are the specific settings and place names Williams uses throughout his poetry; not that everything must be identified, but that real names and specific locales contribute to a poem's immediacy, in addition to being, for most modern readers, more evocative than old-fashioned allusions to mythical places like Xanadu or Arcady. In general, reading "January Morning" with the class, with close attention to Williams's poetic choices—despite his self-proclaimed "indiscriminate" attractions, he is in fact highly discriminating as a poet—can help students see that the poem's variety is a vital part of its remaining fresh and compelling from beginning to end.

I have found that the differences between Williams's style—including the look of his poems on the page—and the more orderly arrangements of the majority of poems students encounter in their anthologies often stimulate them to experiment, and in some cases encourage students who were disinclined to write poetry at all. In either case, the important thing is to experience the sheer excitement of writing poems. As a bonus, once students begin to pay close attention to a poem like "January Morning" and try to assimilate some of its qualities into their own writing, they begin to find a wide range of poetry accessible to them as readers and, in turn, find themselves inspired by it as writers.

Notes

1. William Carlos Williams, *The Collected Poems of William Carlos Williams, Volume I,* A. Walton Litz and Christopher McGowan, eds. (New York: New Directions, 1986), p. 92.

2. Ibid., p. 100.

Reed Bye

William Carlos Williams
Excited by the Actual

William Carlos Williams wrote most of his poems in a free verse based on rhythms he heard in the speech around him. He derived a loose meter for his poems from these spoken rhythms instead of using traditional verse meters because, he said, "There is a natural sense of measure in any language, not precise, not easily set down for study, but there nevertheless. . . . This is the foundation of its prosody."[1] To bring these rhythms into verse, Williams broke phrases and sentences into lines that conveyed the pace and hesitations of speech set against the conventions of grammatical syntax. The poem below, "To a Solitary Disciple," is an early attempt by Williams at this kind of free-verse prosody. In the poem, the speaker, a master or teacher of some sort, is giving advice to a student on how to look at things in order to see them in a more vibrant way. And, although it is never said, the fact that this advice is given in the form of a poem might imply that this vibrancy has something to do with Williams's ideas about writing poetry as well as seeing.

To a Solitary Disciple

Rather notice, mon cher,
that the moon is
tilted above
the point of the steeple
than that its color
is shell-pink.

Rather observe
that it is early morning
than that the sky
is smooth
as a turquoise.

Rather grasp
how the dark
converging lines

of the steeple
meet at the pinnacle—
perceive how
its little ornament
tries to stop them—

See how it fails!
See how the converging lines
of the hexagonal spire
escape upward—
receding, dividing!
—sepals
that guard and contain
the flower!

Observe
how motionless
the eaten moon
lies in the protecting lines.

It is true:
in the light colors
of morning
brown-stone and slate
shine orange and dark blue.

But observe
the oppressive weight
of the squat edifice!
Observe
the jasmine lightness
of the moon.

Notice the imperative verbs opening each stanza (except the second-to-last): *notice, grasp, observe*, and so on. As separate instructions to the student, the stanzas form a rhythmic pattern keyed by these imperatives. But what is the gist of the instructions?

In each of the first three stanzas, the student is told to see things in one way instead of another. For instance, instead of noting that the color of the moon is "shell-pink," or that its texture is "smooth as a turquoise," the student is advised to notice that it is "tilted above / the point of the steeple" and that the time is "early morning." Why? Aren't those first two qualities (color and texture) and their metaphorical associations interesting and engaging? Don't they, in fact, do just the thing we expect poetry to do: bring out the feelings of experience through imaginative comparisons in language? But the speaker seems to be pointing to a different degree of intensity brought to the way we look at things. His advice to the disciple boils down to something like: Look through the superficial qualities of things, and even through the often interesting and beautiful associations they suggest. They are significant, yes, but that is not enough. To really see, you must look into the active *relation* between things. Instead of simply noticing the shell-pink moon, see and feel how it is tilted above the church steeple in the morning sky. In this way you can imaginatively enter the energetic play of the shifting world, rather than simply stand back and describe things as if they existed independently of one another.

In stanzas three and four, the "disciple" (who could also be the reader) is instructed to look even beyond what the eyes perceive and to imagine the vector-lines of the hexagonal steeple extending up through the ornament (perhaps a copper ball or cross) at its pinnacle into a three-dimensional "V" in the space above. The verbs become more energetic: the steeple lines *meet* at the ornament, and though the ornament *tries* to stop them, they *escape* upward. Once such dynamic relations are perceived and felt, associations with other things may also arise in the imagination of the observer, enlivening the image: the image of the moon above the church steeple immediately suggests a flower tilted on its stem. It is a vivid but a momentary impression; the light will change as the sun rises higher and the moon will move from its position above the steeple, perhaps into a noticeable relation with something else, such as the edge of a cloud or the branch of a tree.

The poem's emphasis on looking into active relations among things is reflected in its prosody. The line breaks affect the pacing of the phrases, helping articulate the subject matter and mood of the spoken instruction. Sometimes line breaks interrupt the normal syntactic units in a sentence and sometimes they match them. In the first stanza, for example, the lines, "that the moon is / tilted above / the point of the steeple," offset the normal syntactic divisions ("that the moon / is tilted / above the point / of the steeple"). In doing so, the lines don't rest as stable segments but push on to succeeding lines and give an immediate sense to the "tilted" image. In the fifth stanza, on the other hand, the lines, "Observe / how motionless / the eaten moon / lies in its protecting lines," match the normal divisions of syntax and slow the tempo of the sentence so the image comes forward at a relaxed, step-by-step pace.

In the next stanza, the speaker points out that the morning sun on the slate roof and brownstone walls of the church has actually altered their usual colors. Ordinarily we see a lot of the things around us without really looking at them, missing our actual experience by assuming that the world is a far more fixed place than it really is. If, as I have suggested, this is a poem about poetry as well as perception, the speaker may also be implying that to express ourselves in a poem requires speech or writing that is in tune with the shifts and movement of our real perceptions.

The final stanza of the poem is an especially good example of how attentiveness to our actual experience can convey, with surprising immediacy, the physical and emotional sense of what we are seeing and feeling:

> But observe
> the oppressive weight
> of the squat edifice!
> Observe
> the jasmine lightness
> of the moon.

There is a heavy feel to the sound of the first three lines. Why does the poet choose the word *edifice* instead of *building* or *church*? If you say the lines aloud you can feel the rolling out of the slow, weighty syllables. Your body may even begin to sink a little as you say them.

The next three lines offer the poem's final advice:

> Observe
> the jasmine lightness
> of the moon.

Compare the feel of these last three lines to the three before by reading all six lines aloud. What feeling are you left with at the end?

For me, the contrast is palpable: after the "oppressive weight of the squat edifice" brings our attention down to earth, the "jasmine lightness of the moon" lifts it gently into the morning sky. This is the quality of feeling that really looking at things in their active relation with each other can impart, and which the poem has been encouraging us to notice with its instructions.

Note that here at the end the poem uses the kind of metaphorical imagery it seemed to reject at the beginning. Speaking of the "jasmine lightness" of the moon doesn't seem very different from speaking of its "shell-pinkness." But, again, the difference lies in perceiving the vibrant relations between church, sky, and moon rather than seeing or presenting them as independent things. In these relations, the speaker seems to be saying, lies the exciting energy that we can look into and express in poetry.

Below are two exercises that may help cultivate this kind of attention to active relations among things.

1. Have your students take a fifteen- to twenty-minute walk. Tell them to walk alone without speaking and just be with all the sights, sounds, and smells of the walk. The students should not be told that anything in particular will be asked of them after the walk, but simply to keep their senses awake and not think too much. When they come back to the classroom, they should take their seats, still without talking for a minute or two, until they are settled. Then instruct them as briefly as possible to write down the most vivid image from the walk that remains in their minds, however simple or commonplace it might be. They should take only a minute or two to do this. Then ask them to elaborate on that image and include some elements of the place in which it was perceived: other things around it, the light in the air, etc. Ask next if they can use any verbs to express or show any sense of activity or relationship between these elements. Recommend that they look again at the scene, in the "mind's eye." The whole exercise might take five to ten minutes.

Then ask them to recall another vivid image, and see if something else from the walk comes up, and locate it in its original place and field of sensed relations as concretely as necessary to get its original energy across.

2. Have each student pick three small objects from among things in their desks or in the room and arrange them in front of them. There is no need for the objects to be unusual; pencils, erasers, a Chap Stick, a juice container, etc. will be fine. In fact, the more ordinary the objects the better, to avoid the distracting flash of an unusual object. When these

have been arranged, have the students step back from the arrangement and see if they like its "feel" or want to adjust it. After one adjustment, the arrangement should not be altered again. The students should then begin to write, feeling the relations between the objects as if together they made up an active scene or landscape. They could forget the names and normal uses of the objects. As in Williams's poem, these relations have something to do with direction, shape, weight, and color. The point is to get imaginatively into the arrangement and feel what transpires between the objects in the way Williams seems to be recommending in his poem.

Note

1. "To Write American Poetry." *Fantasy* 5.1 (1935): 12–14.

Gary Lenhart

Stretching Exercises

Range of Motion and Emotion in Four Poems
By William Carlos Williams

I would like to talk about four poems by William Carlos Williams that I have used to teach creative writing to college students, with sometimes exhilarating, sometimes discouraging results. By describing my checkered experience, I hope to broaden what is becoming the received portrait of Williams as an imagist poet, to emphasize the heterogeneous and lively qualities of his poems, to explore some limits of classroom or workshop exercises, and to consider why our enthusiasms don't always fire up our students.

At age forty Williams wrote to his friend Marianne Moore, "You know I began with portraits of old women in bed and the rest of it, and it all seemed very important. Now there has been a quieter, more deliberate composition."[1] I often begin undergraduate workshops by giving students an opportunity to start where Williams did, moving on to "more deliberate composition" later. The two "old women in bed" poems that I use are "Portrait of a Woman in Bed" and "The Last Words of My English Grandmother."

For the purposes of teaching writing, the great virtue of these poems is that they contain speakers who are clearly not the poet. Too often, students view poems as statements created by people who are more sensitive than others. Williams differs from most of the major modernist poets in his fervent, almost spiritual commitment to democracy, i.e., the worth of human experience on its own terms. He does not look down on his audience or his immigrant patients, but directly at them; he listens attentively to other voices and uses those voices in his poems.

Portrait of a Woman in Bed

There's my things
drying in the corner:
that blue skirt
joined to the grey shirt—

I'm sick of trouble!
Lift the covers
if you want me
and you'll see
the rest of my clothes—
though it would be cold
lying with nothing on!

I won't work
and I've got no cash.
What are you going to do
about it?
—and no jewelry
(the crazy fools)

But I've got my two eyes
and a smooth face
and here's this! look!
it's high!

There's brains and blood
in there—
my name's Robitza!
Corsets
can go to the devil—
and drawers along with them—
What do I care!

My two boys?
—they're keen!
Let the rich lady
care for them—
they'll beat the school
or
let them go to the gutter—
that ends trouble.

This house is empty
isn't it?
Then it's mine
because I need it.
Oh, I won't starve
while there's the Bible
to make them feed me.

Try to help me
if you want trouble
or leave me alone—
that ends trouble.

The country physician
is a damned fool
and you
can go to hell!

You could have closed the door
when you came in;
do it when you go out.
I'm tired.

This poem presents an occasion to discuss unreliable narrators, especially important to students raised on movies and television, media heav-
ily dominated by third-person omniscient narratives. I remind students
that the narrator in a poem or story isn't always the author, and that we
may find the narrator to be disagreeable or deluded. Mrs. Robitza in
"Portrait of a Woman in Bed" is an exemplary case. Her shamelessness,
ingratitude, class and religious biases, and irresponsible maternity make
her an unattractive character, particularly to younger students, who are
less apt to admire her perverse vitality than mature readers. Of course,
the speakers in many student poems can be unattractive too, and the
teacher should be careful about criticizing them. I have found myself
more than once gently deriding the persona of a student poem for being
harsh or unsympathetic, only to have the innocent student defend the
speaker with a vehement "But that's me!" I knew that, but assumed the
student would understand I was trying to be tactful. So it's important to
establish early the possibility of discussing the speaker from the distance
of literary narrator or protagonist, and this poem provides a perfect
occasion.

We discuss the details Williams uses to portray the woman in bed. I
ask students what they can know of the speaker from her few utterances.
It's clear to most that she is poor and sick, but they don't understand why
she "won't work." Often they are confused by the lines

But I've got my two eyes
and a smooth face
and here's this! look!

it's high!

There's brains and blood
in there—

And the threat of nudity makes some suspect her character. But the
lines that disturb students most are

My two boys?
—they're keen!
Let the rich lady
care for them—
they'll beat the school
or
let them go to the gutter—
that ends trouble.

and

Oh, I won't starve
while there's the Bible
to make them feed me.

Here's a woman who callously abandons her own sons. Some students find it even worse that she cynically uses the Bible to force people
to support her. Students are also offended by the crudity of her talk,
which is not just impolite, but disrespectful to the person to whom she
is speaking. Many students don't understand why anyone would want to
write about a character such as this. A good question at this point is,
"Doesn't anyone see virtue in speaking honestly? Won't you at least give
her credit for being direct?" If you are dealing with adult students, a few
will agree. But if your students are stuck in the difficult transitions of
adolescence, where they may be struggling to come to terms with their
own feelings, they may resist fiercely the notion that these are anyone's
true feelings. "She's just ill and tired," perhaps "a victim of the classism
in our society." I remind students that anything we know about the character is gained directly from her lips.

Then we read "The Last Words of My English Grandmother."

The Last Words of My English Grandmother

There were some dirty plates
and a glass of milk
beside her on a small table
near the rank, disheveled bed—

Wrinkled and nearly blind
she lay and snored
rousing with anger in her tones
to cry for food,

Gimme something to eat—
They're starving me—
I'm all right—I won't go
to the hospital. No, no, no

Give me something to eat!
Let me take you
to the hospital, I said
and after you are well

you can do as you please.
She smiled, Yes
you do what you please first
then I can do what I please—

Oh, oh, oh! she cried
as the ambulance men lifted
her to the stretcher—
Is this what you call

making me comfortable?
By now her mind was clear—
Oh you think you're smart
you young people,

she said, but I'll tell you
you don't know anything.
Then we started.
On the way

we passed a long row
of elms. She looked at them
awhile out of
the ambulance window and said,

What are all those
fuzzy-looking things out there?
Trees? Well, I'm tired
of them and rolled her head away.

Although "The Last Words of My English Grandmother" contains description and a narrator who may be the author, it also contains an exemplary passage in somebody else's voice. First, we try to distinguish who speaks which lines (not always clear to students confused by the absence of quotation marks). Then we discuss the relationship between the speakers—a grandchild and his or her dying English grandmother. I have been asked, "How do you know that?" I begin with the title, emphasizing its important function in this poem, then read carefully through the first exchanges.

In their book *Poetry Everywhere,* Jack Collom and Sheryl Noethe describe how they use this poem as the basis of a "last words" assignment. I mention that to students as one way to handle my assignment: to write in someone else's voice. I suggest that this task is easiest with someone whose speech patterns are distinctive. It may be someone they met fleetingly, or someone whose voice they know so well that they can hear it at the very mention of the person's name. But there should be some difference in speech or personality to distinguish the poem's persona from the author.

It's remarkable how often, early in the course, this brings out the students with the most agile imaginations. As compared with the repugnant stranger of "Portrait of a Woman in Bed," students find it much easier to write about a parent or grandparent who died, though seldom do they write about it with as much distance as Williams. They tend to sentimentalize the relationship and the attitude of the dying toward life and death. But a few are always emboldened to write honestly and unflinchingly. In one class, I received two terrific poems from this assignment. The first, from a woman whose companion's father was dying of cancer, captured sympathetically the ornery, salty, logging-camp speech of the dying man. The other was by a student who had joined the first for a cigarette break the week before, and had listened to her complaints. The second poem captured the commingled sorrow, boredom, and fatigue of the family member whose life has been disrupted by daily visits to the hospital.

"The Last Words of My English Grandmother" also lends itself to a lesson about revision. Williams published three accounts of this event, a prose version in *The Great American Novel* (and reprinted in *I Wanted to Write a Poem*), and two poems now included in *The Collected Poems*. With advanced students I distribute copies of all three, withholding dates to prevent any assumptions about progression. We then compare them, with particular attention to line breaks, stanzas, use of detail, deletions, the unreliability of memory, and the artifice of anecdote.

•

Two Williams poems that I have introduced to workshops with mixed success are "Impromptu: The Suckers" and "Choral: The Pink Church." I do not use these poems with beginning classes, but introduce them toward the end of poetry workshops with advanced students. Most students know Williams only as the author of straightforward descriptive imagist poems like "The Red Wheelbarrow." I would like them to understand that such is only part of the picture, that he also wrote poems that inspire comparison to the long, shaggy compositions of Philip Whalen, the grand romantic epics of Frank O'Hara, and the obsessive meanderings of Bernadette Mayer, and that poems may be capacious vessels that will hold whatever the imagination touches.

The first problem with "Impromptu: The Suckers" and "Choral: The Pink Church" is that they now require historical introductions. That wasn't true thirty years ago, when Sacco and Vanzetti (in "Impromptu") were still household words. In "The Pink Church," few students recognize William James, John Dewey, Alfred North Whitehead, or martyred Spanish physician (and Williams's patron saint) Michael Servitus. More recognize Poe, Whitman, and Baudelaire. Most know of John Milton, but are flabbergasted to find him "singing like a Communist." It may also be necessary to provide some background about Cold War politics in the U.S. immediately following World War II. Fortunately, Christopher MacGowan's notes in the current edition of *The Collected Poems* provide sufficient background for both poems.

"Impromptu: The Suckers" is the easier of the two for students. In it, Williams rages at all those complicit in the execution of the Italian anarchists. His poem is a litany of accusations, described by Allen Ginsberg elsewhere in this book as "a really prophetic sort of anti-police-state radical rant." (The entire poem is quoted in Ginsberg's essay.) I remember how astounded I was the first time I read the following stanza:

> But after all, the thing that swung heaviest
> against you was that you were scared when
> they copped you. Explain that you
> nature's nobleman! For you know that every
> American is innocent and at peace in his
> own heart. He hasn't a damned thing to be
> afraid of. He knows the government is for
> him. Why, when a cop steps up and grabs
> you at night you just laugh and think it's
> a hell of a good joke—

My students wonder aloud at Dr. Williams's bad humor. One of my most accomplished poets responded to this poem by complaining that "Williams tries too hard to shock his readers." And there is often one student who believes that if Sacco and Vanzetti were anarchists, then why be so angry about their execution? Most students, however, don't disagree with the indictment of injustice expressed by Williams; they simply don't seem to be outraged or surprised by it. Whether at the community college or in the Ivy League, three decades of constant political scandal has inured most contemporary students to this sort of thing. The general attitude is: why does Williams blame the society for the misdeeds of its politicians? They understand his anger at the hypocritical "high-minded / and unprejudiced observers," but resist the rage that erupts into

> Take it out in vile whiskey, take it out
> in lifting your skirts to show your silken
> crotches . . .
> It's no use, you are Americans, just the dregs.
> It's all you deserve. You've got the cash,
> what the hell do you care . . .

I ask them to write their own angry litanies, and as they are generally eager to please, they do. But their anger doesn't erupt; it is borrowed, for the sake of the exercise. I have heard students muttering about politicians with such contempt that I still suppose this might be an outlet for real emotion, but so far we have had neither the inflammatory occasion nor the social analysis to produce good, angry poems.

I like to think that students take from the assignment an appreciation of how anger sustained the rant at fever pitch, that the length of "Impromptu: The Suckers" pushes them to stretch their muscles—or at least their stanzas—and that they see expanded possibilities for subject matter. Yet maybe I have learned more than they. Later in one term, when we read Allen Ginsberg's "Howl," some students were visibly excited and agreed that the poem was "on fire." Nevertheless they quickly assured me that they could never write in that vein. One said, "That may have been okay for then, but things have changed too much." As Williams might have reminded me, a new world demands new poetic practices.

In "Choral: The Pink Church" the problem is the brusque juxtaposition of its range of references. It's simple to go through the poem clarifying allusions, but it's more difficult to explain connections that are never explicit. What can we make of the allusions in this poem: dawn in Galilee, Aeschylus, three popular philosophers, a Spanish martyr who advocated religious tolerance but refused to renounce his Catholicism under pain of death, two French novelists (Proust and Gide) and three mid-nineteenth-century poets (two American and one French), drunks, prostitutes, the aberrant, a virgin's nipple? For me, this grand romantic chorus has always seemed a song of artistic and sexual liberation, a paean to those who stand up against cruelty, oppression, and intolerance, all culminating in a grand chorus echoing Beethoven:

Joy! Joy!
—out of Elysium!

in which even the "unrhymer" Milton would find room to sing "among / the rest . . . like a Communist."

The incoherences of the poem are inextricable from the grandness of its ambition. Williams is in the middle of his epic *Paterson* at this time, and, at sixty years old, heading into new territory. His doctor son has yet to be discharged from the military, and Williams is caring for both his own and his son's patients. We know from his letters that he responded anxiously to the increased political instability that resulted from the atom bomb and the beginning of the Cold War.

Williams reacts against this press of literary, personal, and social demands by grasping in many directions. He wants to address the threatened post-war world, but has yet to finish with a complex group of abstractions that had obsessed him for years. In many ways, the poem presents ideas about things, reversing Williams's own credo. His customary impatience with literary convention combines with his sense of urgency to produce a brisk shorthand that resembles the method of Ezra Pound's *Cantos*, but with more improvisation and larger leaps. He is still working out a vision of a new mongrel world being whelped. The heroes of Williams's pantheon do not wear the mantle of received authority that Pound's or T. S. Eliot's figures wear. Like everything in Williams, they remain quick and elusive, irreducible because they are as multidimensional as life.

What is the writing assignment? After we read the Williams poem with Frank O'Hara's "Ode to Joy," I ask students to compose a poem that might be sung in celebration, an ode to joy. It may be assembled from bits and pieces, and doesn't have to be logical. Indeed, in the vision from Keats that Williams and O'Hara inherited, the joy that surrounds things of beauty also liberates us from the cold eye of common sense.

I don't expect students to compose large masterpieces within the two weeks allotted for this assignment, and the poems I have received from it have been modest. But the quicksilver dartings of Williams's imagination can be liberating to students constrained by traditional notions of narrative. I encourage them to be reckless, to open their celebratory songs to whatever attracts them. As they struggle to shape the hodgepodge that often results, they learn that writing poems is not only a craft to be mastered, but also an exciting experiment with unpredictable results.

Note
1. William Carlos Williams, *The Selected Letters of William Carlos Williams*, John C. Thirlwall, ed. (New York: New Directions, 1984), p. 57.

Barbara Flug Colin

Making a Difference

The Poems of William Carlos Williams as Models for Comparison

For eight years I have been teaching creative writing at the Henry Viscardi School, a pre-K through high school for physically challenged students. Recently, reviewing portfolios of poems written over the years by particular students, I came to realize that studying related works of art had created in these students an awareness of different ways of saying the same thing.

For example, when studying the paintings of Joan Miró, we saw how his *Dutch Interior 1, 1928* broke seventeenth-century artistic conventions in his reinterpretation of H. M. Sorgh's *The Lute Player, 1661*. When we looked at paintings by Degas, Cézanne, and Monet, we also read excerpts from their diaries and letters. Before a visit to a Kandinsky show we compared his paintings, the poems in his book *Klänge*, and music by Scriabin and Schönberg. When we read William Blake's "The Tyger," we looked at his artwork and listened to a modern rendition of the poem by the singing group, Tangerine Dream. Before a visit to a Monet show, we compared his paintings of Antibes and Bordighera to Maupassant's verbal descriptions of those areas in his book *Sur l'eau*. We compared Monet's *Railroad Bridge in Argenteuil* to Renoir's painting of the same scene. (One class poem ended, "The Monet bridge looks whole. / The Renoir bridge looks deserted / like someone cleaned out the colors of the world.")

Such comparisons create discourse: opinions, votes, excited discussions of music, paintings, and poems. No matter how young the class, children have opinions. Engaging with different points of view makes students look harder, see more acutely, and express themselves better. They begin to develop taste and a discernment of the artist's techniques and strategies.

It's a lesson of discovering without "teaching."

The poetry of William Carlos Williams offers other good opportunities for such discoveries. For example, the two versions of his poem "The Locust Tree in Flower" point up his excisions and additions, as well as decisions about line breaks.

The Locust Tree in Flower
[*First version*]

Among
the leaves
bright

green
of wrist-thick
tree

and old
stiff broken
branch

ferncool
swaying
loosely strung—

come May
again
white blossom

clusters
hide
to spill

their sweets
almost
unnoticed

down
and quickly
fall

[*Second version*]

Among
of
green

stiff

old
bright

broken
branch
come

white
sweet
May

again

At first "The Locust Tree in Flower" is difficult to understand. I ask for a volunteer to read each version. Usually there are many volunteers, so there are many readings of each version. Between each I ask leading questions about the number of words in a line, the size and number of stanzas, the excisions, and how the poem looks. Sometimes, using the information the poem gives line by line, I "paint" a picture on the blackboard, so we can see what something "wrist-thick" might refer to and where the broken branch might be. We discuss the value of making up words like "ferncool," and why such delightful inventions might be deleted.

"Which version do you like better?"

Eleventh grader Nick said, "The second version leaves me flat. I like the first better because you can actually put a picture into your mind and think about what's going on."

Shalom said, "The second leaves it to your imagination."

Sometimes I give out "tree" postcards, for example of Corot's tree paintings, and ask students to be like Williams looking at a tree, and to write line by line how they see it. When they're finished, I ask them to go back and put parentheses around words they might leave out. Each student reads both versions to the class, who discuss which version they prefer, and why, as they did with "The Locust Tree in Flower."

Recently Mitchell, who last year as a junior wrote long incomprehensible poems, finished his tree poem first, edited it, and wanted to read first:

Among
the light
and people

its sweets
sort of go
unnoticed
the tree with
finger thinning
branches rises
white blossoms
surround and
camouflage the weightlessness
(of the tree)

Erwin wrote, then edited (his cuts are in parentheses):

Abundance
(It) stands in
groups.

Makes
(the) barren
landscape look

forestful.
Green
puffs

(Something stuck) on
stems.
Giving

radiance (two contrasts)
to (the)
hard earth.

(The) trees
beautiful as
may be

hide something
more exquisite
behind (it)

In a fifth grade class, we read the two versions of Williams's poem, and then I gave each student a postcard of Matisse's paintings *Le Bonheur de Vivre* and *La Danse*. I asked leading questions, beginning with: "How many words did Williams leave out in the second version?" I wrote the answer on the blackboard, as the beginning of a poem, and we discussed where the line break in it might go.

"How many people did Matisse leave out? What else did he leave out?"

Excited, the students called out the last five lines and then, from many suggestions, we voted on a title for our group poem:

Leaving Out

William Carlos Williams left out 21 words
in the second version of "The Locust Tree in Flower."
Matisse left out people from *Le Bonheur de Vivre*
to paint *La Danse.*
He also left out trees, goats, the horizon, figures.
He changed the sky color.
He left out yellow that they're standing in.
And pink, orange and red.
He left out whiter bodies.
The dark blue bark becomes light blue sky in *La Danse.*

Williams's three versions of his poem "The Great Figure" and the Charles Demuth painting *The Figure 5 in Gold* offer other good models for comparison. Here are Williams's three versions:

1.
Among the rain
and lights
I saw the figure 5
gold on red
moving
with weight and urgency
tense
unheeded
to gong clangs
siren howls
and wheels rumbling
through the dark city.

2.
Among the rain
and lights
I saw the figure 5
in gold

on a red
firetruck
moving
with weight and urgency
tense
unheeded
to gong clangs
siren howls
and wheels rumbling
through the dark city.

3.
Among the rain
and lights
I saw the figure 5
in gold
on a red
firetruck
moving
tense
unheeded
to gong clangs
siren howls
and wheels rumbling
through the dark city.

Charles Demuth, Williams's painter friend, modeled his painting *The Figure 5 in Gold* on this poem (see figure opposite). These works show students how visual and verbal languages interrelate and, in this instance, evoke motion and emotion. Demuth's "ray lines" show smaller things further back in the time and space Williams verbally compacts. Demuth presents the synchronous perceptions of rain, streetlights, and city buildings.

Recently, in a grade 5–6 class, I handed out postcards of the Demuth painting and the three versions of "The Great Figure" poem and asked the students what they saw. They saw 5's, the words *No.* and *Bill*, and a ticket (the fire engine).

"What time of day is it?" I asked.

"Night."

"What weather?"

"Rain."

The Figure 5 in Gold by Charles Demuth. The Metropolitan Museum of Art, The Alfred Steiglitz Collection, 1949. (49.59.1)

"Why?"

"The lines."

"If the ticket were something else, what could it be?"

"A truck. A train, see the tracks. . . . A fire truck! . . . C. D. must be Charles Demuth. W. C. W. . . . William Carlos Williams." Excited with discovery, the class heated. They called out: "That five on the fire truck . . . it is moving away . . . No toward, getting closer . . . Fast!"

"What sound would you hear? Can you find words for that sound?"

In another fifth grade class, when we compared the three versions of the poem, everyone wanted to read. We started with versions 1 and 2.

"What is different?"

"'Gold on red' becomes 'in gold / on a red / firetruck.'"

"Why?" I asked.

"To make it clearer."

Then a student read version 3.

"What is different here?"

"He left out 'with weight and urgency.'"

When I asked students from fifth grade through high school to write their own poems based on the Williams and Demuth models, they borrowed techniques from the poems and the painting, but used them with originality:

Among the firetruck
the number five
running its siren
going through the
dark misty night
tall buildings
street lights shining
dark damp roads

   —Erich, seventh grade

Sabrina, a high school student, created a two-line title:

Numbers in the mist
With a white glare

Numbers 555 bill on 555 the street lights dance at you
with happiness. To creep up behind a street sign is to glare
at the street with a rose on the side. And a train across
Broadway.

Other students wrote:

Among three things

Among three Fives

Among three Lights

   —Wanisha, sixth grade

Among three fives
a red wagon
appears
in the sky
I see no stars
   —Dylan, fifth grade

among
of
the
red

fire engine

bringing

the
fireman
to
the
fire

with
the
red

sirens
glowing
in
the
night
and
the
horn
beeping

brump
brump

and

the
fire engine
speeding
toward the

glare
of
the fire

   —*Thomas, fifth grade*

In the discussion of the poem in its own terms, the painting in its terms, and each in terms of the other, the students saw ways of expressing motion and emotion in multiple views. When Jimmy, a sixth grader, said, "I am standing on the sidewalk. It's going by very fast. That's why the painting shows different parts," it reminded me of Williams's description of how he wrote the poem: "As I approached . . . I heard a great clatter of bells and the roar of a fire engine passing at the end of the street down Ninth Avenue. I turned just in time to see a golden figure on a red background flash by. The impression was so sudden and forceful . . . I wrote a poem."[1]

With older students the discussion was more sophisticated. "Why three fives?" I asked eleventh graders.

Carlos said, "To show progressive fives. The smallest, then bigger and bigger, the progression of the size, it's moving back or forward, in at you. It's like someone's life being progressed from young to old, kid to teenager to adult. He's taking fragments of different kinds of experience and combining them. We're all fives."

"Why leave out 'with weight and urgency'?" I asked.

Nick said, "When you say 'tense / unheeded' you don't need 'weight and urgency.'"

I passed out postcards of the Demuth painting. Tommy, despite the gauze over his arms and hands, wrote fast and then wanted to read first, without revising:

Five, pacing back and forth.
Thinking hard. Nowhere to go
except forward and back. So much
noise he can't take it. Five's face
starts to turn red. Wanting the noise
to STOP!!
So bad. Five finally is able to
run from the noise. Five runs so fast
you see three of him. As five gets
away from the noise he calms down

and turns back to his normal color.
Gold.

Note

1. William Carlos Williams, *The Autobiography of William Carlos Williams*, p. 172.

Bibliography

Cézanne, Paul. *Paul Cézanne: Letters.* John Rewald, ed. Marguerite Kay, trans. New York: Hacker Art Books, 1976.

Kandinsky, Wassily. *Klänge (Sounds).* Elizabeth R. Napier, trans. New Haven: Yale University Press, 1981.

Kendall, Richard, ed. *Degas by Himself.* Boston: Little, Brown and Co., 1987.

Maupassant, Guy de. *Sur l'eau (Afloat).* Marlo Johnston, trans. London: Peter Owen, 1995.

White, Barbara Ehrlich. *Impressionists Side by Side.* New York: Alfred A. Knopf, 1996.

Williams, William Carlos. *The Autobiography of William Carlos Williams.* New York: Random House, 1951; New Directions, 1967.

_____. *The Collected Poems.* A. Walton Litz and Christopher Mac-Gowan, eds. New York: New Directions, 1986.

Wilson-Bareau, Juliet, ed. *Manet by Himself.* Boston: Little, Brown and Co., 1991.

Sally Cobau

Images to Stay Awake For
Teaching William Carlos Williams's Pictures from Breughel

After teaching poetry in the schools for two years, I'm starting to learn what works and what doesn't. One poet whose work almost always works well is William Carlos Williams. Williams's gentle, observant, sometimes whimsical poems are wonderful to use because they are full of vivid colors, shapes, and textures. With a doctor's attentiveness, he expertly captures a moment on the brink of change in his spare imagist poems, such as "The Red Wheelbarrow."[*] His succinctness persuades the reader to consider language in a new way; his poems move gracefully from point to point, cinematically scanning the immediate landscape. All these features make his poems accessible and seductive—a good combination for teaching.

The "Brueghel poems," from Williams's Pulitzer Prize-winning collection, *Pictures from Brueghel and Other Poems*, are delightful representations of works by the sixteenth-century Flemish painter Pieter Brueghel, the Elder. These poems rely on the layering of details in Brueghel's work. In comparison to the many somber religious and allegorical paintings of the time, Brueghel's paintings stand out in their sheer rambunctiousness. They focus on the daily life of the peasantry of his time. People laugh and play, work in the fields, and gather together for ceremonies. Dogs run under the tables and lick the bowls of their masters. Children get into mischief. You could almost call some of his paintings obscene in their abundance.

When I first read Williams's Brueghel poems, I was a bit surprised. The excess of Brueghel seemed in such contrast to the pared-down diction of Williams. The poems are William Carlos Williams through and through—they only begin with the paintings. Yet I came to see that the tension created by the contrast in style between the paintings and the writing adds to the poems' interest.

---

[*] The exercise I'm going to describe here focuses on Williams's Brueghel poems, but I want to stress that I do this exercise in coordination with other Williams poems, such as "The Red Wheelbarrow" and "This is Just to Say."

If I had to characterize what Williams was after in these poems, I would say that he was pointing to details that might be overlooked in the Brueghel works. Brueghel included so many small wonders, peculiarities such as a spoon in the hat of one of the wedding party and a crooked sign. Williams devotes three lines to this sign. As with much of Williams's work, these poems seem to be about keen attention to the everyday world.

When I do this exercise in class, I bring in both the paintings (reproduced on postcards) and the poems. I first have the students look closely at one of the Brueghel paintings, say *Hunters in the Snow*, for half a minute. Next I have them recollect what they've seen, making a list on scratch paper. Then we make a collaborative list on the board with everything the kids remember. I urge them to be specific. If a student says, "Hunters walking through the snow," I ask, "How many hunters?" Some students will have observed that there are three hunters, even though the third one is hard to see. Then they add: "There are birds." "There is a bonfire." "The inn has a crooked sign on it." "A woman is walking across a bridge." "There are mountains in the background." Because Brueghel's paintings are so full, everyone sees different things. Then I read the Williams poem aloud:

The Hunters in the Snow

The over-all picture is winter
icy mountains
in the background the return

from the hunt it is toward evening
from the left
sturdy hunters lead in

their pack the inn-sign
hanging from a
broken hinge is a stag a crucifix

between his antlers the cold
inn yard is
deserted but for a huge bonfire

that flares wind-driven tended by
women who cluster
about it to the right beyond

> the hill is a pattern of skaters
> Brueghel the painter
> concerned with it all has chosen
>
> a winter-struck bush for his
> foreground to
> complete the picture   .   .

I have always marveled at how this poem seems to capture equally the ephemeral quality of the moment (the hunters returning, soon it will be dark) and the permanence of art (that Brueghel chooses to use "a winter-struck bush"). The ellipsis points that end the poem seem to indicate that more is happening, but it would be impossible to capture it all. In the lines "Brueghel the painter / concerned with it all has chosen," Williams seems be comparing himself to Brueghel, reflecting on painters' and poets' mutual need to take extreme care with the subjects they choose.

I like to discuss the poem's form with my students: how the ideas blur together, as in the line "from the hunt it is toward evening." I stress that the poem reflects the painting insofar as everything is unified. At the same time, the short lines and stanzas create a lot of white space, which in turn—especially when combined with the pauses and interlocking effect of the enjambment—gives the feeling of a lack of boundaries. I ask my students what qualities they feel the poem and painting share. How are they different? I also ask them why they think Williams chose to write about this particular painting.

Next I read Williams's "Peasant Wedding" (based on Brueghel's *Folk Wedding*):

> Pour the wine bridegroom
> where before you the
> bride is enthroned her hair
>
> loose at her temples a head
> of ripe wheat is on
> the wall beside her the
>
> guests seated at long tables
> the bagpipers are ready
> there is a hound under
>
> the table the bearded Mayor
> is present women in their
> starched headgear are

gabbing all but the bride
hands folded in her
lap is awkwardly silent simple

dishes are being served
clabber and what not
from a trestle made of an

unhinged barn door by two
helpers one in a red
coat a spoon in his hatband

We then spend some time discussing this poem. I point out the vocabulary that clues in the reader that the setting is probably early Renaissance—the starched headgear, the bagpipers, etc. We discuss whether or not the bride in the painting really does seem "awkward."

I then ask the students to write their own poems based on individual Brueghel paintings. I tell them that, like Williams, they should focus on the aspects of the painting that interest them, although they may want to emulate Williams's concision and short lines.

Here are few examples from a group of high school students:

FROM *Hunters in the Snow*

The people scavenge
the darkness
blackness
frosty silence with
footsteps
piling
on the windowpane.
    —*Carli Taylor*

Up in the trees
above the coated town
above the ant-sized people

No one sees the blackbirds
            harbingers of death . . .

    —*Jessie Childress*

•

FROM *Folk Wedding*

Folk Wedding

Dogs blend into the wall
the stick stands out above
spoons are hat placements
and your feathers . . .
eat meat and custard pie

Is there enough for me?
Brides grown up too soon
not in white
but purple and blue
liquid dog under the table
           like you

Hey that's a big bite
sorry, don't know if I like it or not
Wanted a taste
these birds melted under feathers
many years ago
make me choke—smoke, scent, feathers

like a colony
of birds in the sky
a ribbon tying me up
disintegrated
dry complaints

    —*Genevieve Marie Ardrus*

Afterwards, I ask my students to compare Williams's poems with their own. This always brings out some interesting remarks. One student, Jessie, who wrote about *Hunters in the Snow*, felt that the painting has ominous undertones Williams doesn't address. Williams says the hunters are "sturdy," but Jessie thought they look tired. "And look at those scary birds," she said. "The painting is about death."

Finally, I may bring in art books with reproductions of works by Gauguin, Van Gogh, Picasso, and others, and have the students each choose a painting and then write a poem about it. As a variation, I like to bring an assortment of photographs and pictures from magazines (*National Geographic* works well) together with my Brueghel postcards. Having the students combine images and details from two or three distinctly different pictures often gets interesting results.

Bob Blaisdell

How Do You Know When You're in Love?

Teaching "The Knife of the Times"

"The Knife of the Times" is four pages long, 1,149 words. Williams wrote and published it in the late 1920s, and it was based on an experience a woman, "Maura," had told him about. Two women—girlhood friends—grow up, marry, live apart, but write each other letters. Eventually, Ethel realizes she is in love with Maura, in spite of what seems to be, for Ethel, satisfactory marriage and motherhood. When Ethel reveals her feelings, Maura is surprised, but agrees to meet her (after twenty years!) for lunch in New York City. During lunch, Ethel makes advances and begs Maura to come visit her. Maura does not know what to do. She is not in love with Ethel, but she is overwhelmed and flattered.

The first time I read "The Knife of the Times," I was twenty-one, a senior in college. I had already read a volume of Williams's poetry, but I was more thrilled by the prose—this is the first story in *The Farmers' Daughters*, and how beautifully, quickly, and simply it read!

When I first taught "The Knife of the Times" in the mid-1980s, to first-year composition students at the University of California, Santa Barbara, many of them took Ethel's revelation personally, as practically an assault on proper and fitting feelings. They squawked and squirmed, but their reactions were mild compared with the confident condemnation of poor Ethel by my students in New York City, where I taught for three years at Borough of Manhattan Community College (I currently teach at Kingsborough Community College in Brooklyn).

Sometimes, particularly with first-year composition classes, I like to start by reading a story without saying anything beforehand. I just hand out copies, stand or sit in front of them, and begin reading aloud. And this is what I did that day, my first month of teaching in New York.

I read: *As the years passed the girls who had been such intimates as children still remained true to one another.*

Samuel, an upright, married, thirty-five-year-old Haitian immigrant who liked to sit in the front row, served as a self-appointed Greek chorus. He was good about murmuring long, thoughtful "Mmms" to various points I made. He also had a particularly flattering "Ahh, yes, I see!" Samuel was almost always attentive, or attentive-seeming. When I got to *Until at last the secret was out. It is you, Maura, that I want. Nothing but you. Nobody but you can appease my grief,* Samuel exclaimed, "Oh, my!"

Martha, a matronly native of rural Jamaica, sucked her teeth in disgust, and then said, "Woo, boy!"

When I read *She spoke of her longings, to touch the velvet flesh of her darling's breasts, her thighs,* a few women exclaimed with audible huffs. One said, "Yuck!"

I glanced about the room and read on. The men, who made up a third of the twenty-odd students, were less expressive: they were, it seemed, dumbfounded.

The ending has never failed to elicit a kind of panic among the students: *What shall I do? thought Maura afterward on her way home, on the train alone. Ethel had begged her to visit her, to go to her, to spend a week at least with her, to sleep with her. Why not?*

"Why not?!" burst out Elvira. "What's she mean, 'Why not?'!"

"She means 'Why not?' That is, maybe yes, maybe no. What's that mean when you say it?"

"When I say it? It means I'm gonna do it! But I don't say it to no friend of mine if she asks me to sleep with her!"

"Maura doesn't say it to Ethel," I said. (In *I Wanted to Write a Poem,* Williams remarked that "to find a woman telling me about her experience intrigued me. She was not shocked, just amazed. The women remained friends. . . ."[1])

"She says it to herself," said Adeyinka, an eighteen-year-old native of Lagos. "She's *thinking* about it—no more than that. Correct, professor?"

"Right."

A few of the women got upset. "Thinking about it! She shouldn't do no thinking about it!" said Camille.

"Just yes or no?" I asked.

"Yes!" said Camille. "I mean, no! She shouldn't think yes for a second."

"Because if she does? . . . What are you saying?"

She shook her head. "Don't think twice."

"Are you mad at Maura?"

"If Ethel said that to me, I swear I'd punch her in the face!"

The men howled! I shook my head. "So you hate Ethel? She threatens you? She doesn't threaten Maura."

"'Cause Maura don't know which way is up," said Camille.

Elvira chipped in: "I pity Ethel!"

"For what?"

"For being in love with me."

"She's not in love with you."

"With *Maura*, okay?"

"Okay," I said. "But what if a man you didn't want to go out with, a friend of many years, a guy friend, what if he told you he was in love with you?"

Elvira shook her head. "Won't happen!"

"Why not?"

"My boyfriend don't let me have no guy friends," said Elvira. After a short, awkward silence, she added, "If I wanted one I could."

Camille called out, "I know, I know! Because . . . this happened to me!"

"With a woman?" asked Samuel.

"No, with a man!" said Camille. "He was my friend, and then when me and my boyfriend broke up, he came out. He came out like Ethel."

"And what'd you do?"

"I shouldn't say!" she laughed.

"What?!" nearly everybody asked.

"It was like I thought to myself, 'Why not?'"

Now the men laughed—not in the least anxious, but excited and interested.

"Pardon me for asking," said Roman, "but what happened?"

"No!" said Camille. "This isn't no talk show where they pay you to tell on yourself."

"The Bible," said Rosemarie, interrupting, and weighing her pause, "says same and same sex is wrong."

"Sure," I answered, "but it says a lot of things. It also says to be tolerant. Anyway. . . ."

We took a breather, and I began telling the students about how the story had been written by a family doctor, not far across the Hudson

River, nearly seventy years before. "Think of your grandmother's time—or your great-grandmother's. And now think about us. We're *aware* of homosexual feelings, and relationship possibilities, and we have or learn tolerance of other kinds of relationships in a way Maura and Ethel, at least at first, haven't."

"It's wicked!" said Rosemarie.

"Isn't it love that Ethel feels?"

"No," said Rosemarie. "No. Not if she feels that for women."

"You see, professor, that's two *women*," explained Samuel.

"Yeah, sure, I know. Let me reread where Ethel's talking about her feelings."

"Don't!" laughed Christina.

"No, I will." I read: *Ethel told her about her children, how she had had one after the other—to divert her mind, to distract her thoughts from their constant brooding. Each child would raise her hopes of relief, each anticipated delivery brought only renewed disappointment. She confided more and more in Maura. She loved her husband; it was not that. In fact, she didn't know what it was save that she, Ethel, could never get her old friend Maura out of her mind.* Then I said, "Sounds like love to me."

"But it's *disgusting*," said Sharine. Sharine was one of only four students in this class born and raised in the United States. She was heavy-set, young, and had a girlish manner and voice.

"What if Ethel were thinking about a man?" I said, thinking I'd trapped her.

"It'd still be disgusting," she said.

But the class gave her some argument.

"Ethel's just mixed up," said Nilda. "It's not disgusting, it's just her feelings are misplaced."

"All right," I said, "but Ethel's not mixed up. She was mixed up for twenty years. Finally, after agonizing forever, she figures out that she's in love. She doesn't want to be in love with a woman, with her friend, but she is."

"Then I feel sorry for her."

"Yeah, so do I—but just in the way that I feel sorry for somebody who falls in love with someone they think they 'shouldn't' fall in love with. Can anybody choose who they fall in love with?"

"No," said Samuel, brightening, "I don't think so."

"So don't you feel sympathy for Ethel? She didn't decide to fall in love with Maura, right? And this is . . . seventy years ago! She hasn't got any kind of social support. She's really out on her own."

"Yes," nodded Samuel. "I agree with you, professor . . . wholeheartedly. Still, if you don't mind my saying, I think she should have kept feelings like that to herself."

"Yeah!" said Sharine. "It's not that I don't like gay people, it's just . . ." —she turned to the class to appeal—"wouldn't that be terrible if she was your friend and she told you something like this?" Now she smiled at me: "How would you like it if your best friend was in love with you?"

I laughed. "I'd feel bad for her."

"Her!"

"Yeah, my best friend's a woman."

"Your wife?"

"Well . . . no. I know there's that 'My wife's my best friend' thing, but I don't mean that."

"So your best guy-buddy! What about him?"

"I don't know."

"You wouldn't feel betrayed?"

"Betrayed? No!"

"No?" said Samuel, with a worried expression.

"No. Don't friends fall in love all the time?"

"No," said Sharine.

"All right, then, with guys and women, ones who are friends?"

"Well, sometimes."

"That's true!" said Samuel, nodding.

"So, anyway, you don't get to choose who you fall in love with, do you?"

I told them a story about myself, about having been in love with a woman named Denise, who went out with me, but didn't love me. I started to go out with another woman, Sandra, who did seem to love me. Sandra and I would've made a good match. "I should've been—I would've liked to have been—in love with Sandra, but I wasn't."

"I see," said Samuel. "And what happened with the first one?"

"Nothing. Denise and I stopped going out. Then we became good friends. That's what she—Denise—and I should've been all along, except that I was in love with her."

"I see."

"We're going to write today."

"I'm not writing about this story," said Sharine.

"You won't write directly about it. All I want to know is—and you can do this in any form you like: a list, a story, a 'scientific' analysis, whatever—How do you know when you're in love?"

"'How do you know?'" asked Sharine.

"Right. How do you know?"

"You're trying to show us, right, professor?" asked Samuel.

"Show what?"

"That we know, in ourselves, what Ethel is feeling. Yes?"

I shrugged, smiling. "Okay, so go ahead. *How do you know when you're in love?*"

"Can it be a poem?" asked Sharine.

"Sure."

"A song?"

"All right. So go ahead, in the next ten or fifteen minutes, tell me—tell us, because I'll read all these aloud today—how you know when you're really in love."

"And not just lusting!" said Samuel, who as soon as he said this seemed to blush.

"Right!" I said. "When can you tell it's love and not horniness?"

"Men don't know the difference," said devout Rosemarie.

"We don't?" I asked.

The women laughed, and Nilda said, "Some men do!"

"Men don't know the difference," insisted Rosemarie. "They say 'love,' but they don't know what it is."

"Come on, you guys," I said. "You're going to let that go unchallenged?" At this encouragement, the men averted their eyes or went stone-faced. "Anyway, everybody write about how you know you're in love, even if other people say it's lust."

Note

1. William Carlos Williams, *I Wanted to Write a Poem: The Autobiography of the Works of a Poet*. Reported and edited by Edith Heal (New York: New Directions, 1978), p. 50.

David Surface

Using "The Use of Force"

A few years ago I spent some weeks as visiting writer at a small college in northern Ohio. The students seemed intelligent, reasonably well-to-do, comfortable with themselves. Their ideas about literature, which boiled down to the eternal outcry of the twenty-year-old, needed shaking up. So when one young man leaned back in his chair, crossed his arms, and asked who *I* thought they should read, I explained that I couldn't tell them which writer would wake them up and help open the world for them—I could only tell them who had done the same for me.

The first time I read the fiction of William Carlos Williams it was a tattered gray library copy of *Knife of the Times*, a collection of stories like I'd never read before. The voice on the page was like a knife cutting through everything that felt dead and difficult about writing. The rapid-fire, staccato sentences, the quotation marks that had fallen away or been burned off by the sheer speed of the writing, the refusal to tidy up experience by smoothing off its rough edges, all seemed to come from a mind that was as impatient as I was with everything artificial about fiction. By the time I'd made it through the first three stories I was laughing out loud, not because the stories were funny (although they often were) but because of the sheer exhilaration of realizing that writing could be like this.

The students' models for "experimental" writing were the usual undergraduate heroes, with Kerouac, Bukowski, and Rimbaud leading the pack. To these young people, lifestyle and subject matter seemed as important as writing style, the more "on-the-edge" the better. So it wasn't strange that many of them found it difficult to recognize Williams as an experimental writer, not just because of the deceptively plainspoken language of his stories, but also because of the middle-class circumstances of the author. Because they took him to be just another traditional, realistic fiction writer, they judged his work the way they would any "normal" American short story. Hence, Williams's jagged endings and breakneck transitions in *Knife of the Times*, which I considered poetic and energizing, the students found confusing or just plain weird. "These aren't stories," was what one young woman said. *Who says?* was the challenge I wanted to throw back at them. I wanted them to see that a story could take many different forms and I wanted them to feel freed by that sense of possibilities. But I realized I needed to find a Williams story that could overcome their objections, one that would fulfill their need for narrative tension while stimulating them to push the boundaries.

In his essay "A Beginning on the Short Story," Williams says, "A novel is many different things, a short story only one." Nowhere is that more brilliantly realized than in his story "The Use of Force." The entire action of the story can be summed up like this: a doctor making a house call tries to make a stubborn little girl open her mouth. Williams turns this simple event into a tour de force by paying attention to *everything* and reporting it as honestly and directly as possible. The story begins in typical Williams fashion:

> They were new patients to me, all I had was the name, Olson. Please come down as soon as you can, my daughter is very sick.

Here you can feel Williams's impatience with the whole expository baggage of "fiction writing": the absence of quotation marks and the borderline run-on punctuation are not affectations—they're the tracks he's left behind in his hurry to get to what really interests him.

Henry James said that "realism, in order to be realism, must take into account the entire field of experience," and that is what Williams does in the following passage:

> The father tried his best, and he was a big man but the fact that she was his daughter, his shame at her behavior and his dread of hurting her made him release her just at the critical moment several times when I had almost achieved success, till I wanted to kill him. But his dread also that she might have the diphtheria made him tell me to go on, go on though he himself was almost fainting, while the mother moved back and forth behind us raising and lowering her hands in an agony of apprehension.

Here you can see Williams's skill at weaving together action, psychological observation, and dialogue into a near-seamless whole. Also typical are his talent for surprising, matter-of-fact admissions that leap off the page, as well as sudden changes of mood (empathizing with the father one moment, then admitting *I wanted to kill him*). These small, startling outbursts are scattered throughout the story:

After all, I had already fallen in love with the savage brat, the parents were contemptible to me. In the ensuing struggle they grew more and more abject, crushed, exhausted while she surely rose to magnificent heights of insane fury of effort bred of her terror of me.

And later:

Feeling that I must get a diagnosis now or never I went at it again. But the worst of it was that I too had got beyond reason. I could have torn the child apart in my own fury and enjoyed it. It was a pleasure to attack her.

Although these could be classified as difficult or even unacceptable thoughts, this is not confessional writing. Williams no more "confesses" these feelings than a radar screen "confesses" the formation of a storm front. It happens, he records it, and moves on. It's this *moving on* that distinguishes Williams from other "psychological" writers who pause in their narratives to provide the reader with insights. Though "The Use of Force" bristles with psychological observations, it never loses forward momentum. This is because, for Williams, there is no separation between thought, feeling, and action. In Williams's work, thought *is* action, feeling *is* action. A man forcing a spoon into a child's mouth, a sudden surge of blind rage—both are physical occurrences, real things happening in the room. And Williams weaves them together within one seemingly minimal framework.

After reading the story aloud in class, I told my students to take one simple action two people are doing together and to write about it from beginning to end. I encouraged them not to step outside of the moment, but to stay inside it and see what happens.

The results were not successful. The students followed the guidelines of the assignment in the most rudimentary way—describing two characters performing one activity together—but did not achieve Williams's dynamic balance of physical and psychological action. Students whose previous work had been action-driven, with little or no internal life, stayed in that vein, while students whose writing had been heavy with psychological and philosophical rhetoric did not bring more physical action into their writing.

I think I was responsible for the students' not "getting" the Williams exercise, partly because I had been so insistent on their seeing his writing as "radical" or "experimental," and because I'd talked too much about his techniques before allowing them to write.

The next time I tried the Williams exercise was in an adult-education course at an arts center in upstate New York. The students there were a mixed group with wildly different backgrounds and tastes in reading. A few seemed familiar with contemporary fiction, while others boasted of having stopped at Hemingway or Dickens. All of them, however, responded to "The Use of Force." For my part, I took care not to prejudice them by labeling Williams as an "experimental" or "modernist" writer; I simply had them read the story out loud in class, then told them what I wanted them to do.

I asked them to choose an experience two people have together, the simpler the better. A father teaching his daughter how to drive. A mother washing her young son's hair. If the experience has a definite beginning and end, that is even better. I told them to tell everything that happens, inside and out. This was tricky because I didn't want them to become bogged down in "confession"; I told them to read the Williams story again and think of it not as confession, but as *reportage*. Most important, I told them to keep moving. "Think of the experience you're writing about as a train," I told them. "You're riding to the end of the line. You may see a lot of interesting things outside the window, you may even make little stops, but you can get off only for a moment before the train starts moving again. Remember to *get back on the train.*"

Even after having read "The Use of Force" a second time, some students remained unconvinced that describing a single, elemental experience could make a good piece of writing; although they had no trouble thinking of simple experiences to write about, a few of them doubted their ability to "stretch it out." I told them not to think of it as "stretching it out," but *breaking it open*. I told them to try the following experiment: go home and put a video on, one you've watched before, a movie or a home video of you and your family. Then watch a few scenes in slow motion. If you've never done this before, you'll be surprised at how many things you've never noticed. After a while, it actually starts to look as if it's a whole different video. People who looked as if they were laughing now look as if they're screaming in pain or anger; people playing football and tackling each other look as if they're caressing. Notice all the new things you see. Play it over and over again if you need to. Then do the same thing when you write your Williams exercise, only this time the "video" you're playing is the memory in your head. And it's also inside you, recording your smallest reaction, thought, and feeling, even those you have trouble identifying.

One young man brought in a piece about helping a disabled girl at summer camp:

> We find ourselves keeping pace. So we move on together, and I notice she's smiling, for real this time. It twists me inside a little. A clockwork half grimace in the arc of her swing. We reach the stairs and she stops dead. She hasn't thought this far ahead. I take her crutch and give her my hand . . . I stand one step below her and she puts her arm around my neck. Her weight is nothing. She and I sweat into each other and her hair tickles my cheek. . . . Marionettes with tangled strings, we lurch and sway all the way down. I help her get in her car, and don't think anything of it. And I can't wait for tomorrow.
>
> —*Jim Keyes*

This piece is remarkable for the easy way it blends unadorned physical statements (*I stand one step below her and she puts her arm around my neck*), more lyrical sentences (*A clockwork half grimace in the arc of her swing*), and the kind of blunt admissions that give Williams's writing its heat and pulse (*It twists me inside a little . . . And I can't wait for tomorrow*).

One young woman brought in a piece about a long car ride with her father:

> He has never had any tolerance for partial information. So I say no, no plans. . . . I sound pathetic to myself and avoid my reflection in the side mirror. In the pause that follows is my father's habit of irritation. A habit he thinks I never pick up on. He is irritated because I have shut him out. And it is my guilty pleasure to pretend I don't notice this.
>
> Sometimes we pass a car that floats as if still as we go by. We are superior to them, whoever they are. The curves we see other cars taking ahead of us stretch out and are disappointingly straight by the time we get there— we barely feel the dips and turns of geography, enclosed within the static noise of the car and our gentle propelling forward, which feels much more like sitting still than it does moving.
>
> —*Jean Kellet*

This piece differs from the last in that the psychological admissions come grouped together at the end of the first paragraph, but it's notatble

99

for the way that the writing turns next to the shared physical qualities of the experience as a way of helping to erase or ease the uncomfortable distance between the two characters, so that, by the end, *he* and *I* have become *we*.

By limiting students' stories to one basic action, the teacher can relieve some students' anxieties over what should happen next (plot), and leave their minds free to wander deeper into areas of thought and feeling that might go ignored in more busily plotted work.

The work of beginning fiction writers tends to suffer from two different syndromes—either it's excessively external and action-focused with little or no internal life, or it's excessively internal in that the psychological insights come tumbling out at random, not grounded in any particular physical reality. Using Williams's method from "The Use of Force" can give new internal depth to the action-obsessed young writer and give solid, down-to-earth grounding to the young writer with his or her head in the clouds.

Jordan Davis

Three Fiction Writing Ideas
From William Carlos Williams's White Mule

White Mule is the greatest novel by a poet this side of Hardy's *Return of the Native*. Following the lessons of realism, naturalism, and imagism—and succumbing to the pieties of none of them—Williams writes pure prose. He has no awful hidden point to make, no bitterness at circumstance, only a continuously shining celebration of things as they happen to be.

The book describes the birth and growth of the baby girl who would grow up and become Williams's wife. It also tells the story of what his future father-in-law, Joe Stecher, a printer and union founder, did during a labor strike. At the same time, Williams reports on the daily life of Joe's wife Gurlie. Of Williams's fiction, *White Mule* shares the most with his poetry that exemplifies his "no ideas but in things" dictum. It also reflects the energy, clinical accuracy, and varying rhythms of the poems. High school and college students will enjoy this book, and it will be useful for some of them as writers.

Ambitious teachers might assign the whole book; it's consistently surprising and plain-spoken about everyday phenomena (childhood illness, weather, problems at work). Teachers short on time could assign the first four chapters (fifty-six pages), in which the baby is born, visitors arrive, Joe spends time at work, and Gurlie runs her household. The assignments that follow are drawn from those chapters.

In the early parts of *White Mule*, the baby does not speak, but Williams makes her as lively as any other character in the novel, partly by describing specifically how she moves and looks around, and partly by describing how everybody reacts to her. Other works with nonspeaking characters include Kafka's "The Metamorphosis" (in which the protagonist is changed into a bug) and Beckett's *Waiting for Godot* (in which the title character is absent), but unlike *White Mule*, these works use absence to create an anxious or depressing mood.

Have your students read the first four chapters of *White Mule*, and discuss with them how Williams creates such a vivid nonspeaking character. Then have them write a story or narrative passage in which the characters are represented equally (in dialogue, in description, in action), but in which at least one of the characters doesn't say anything (or is kept from sight, or in some other way is made absent). There are several ways to "hide" a character—by writing a dialogue and then deleting one person's part; by having the characters play hide-and-seek; or by making some of the characters be forces of nature (e.g., the sun, erosion, love).

•

Joe, the father, is in a more complex position than the baby. He has helped to found the typographer's union (with Samuel Gompers, no less!), but he has become disenchanted with the demands of the union, which seem excessive to the point of dishonesty. We read about his drawing up a bid on a government contract, daydreaming about hunting and fishing in the forests of Germany, crawling around under the presses, standing up to his bosses, and being a little surly when his wife tells him they need to move from their small, cheap apartment to a bigger, more expensive place. When Joe brings the contract bid to his bosses, there is a dramatic pause:

> Joe's got another daughter. That's fine, Mr. Stecher, said the Junior partner. Meanwhile Joe was glad Gurlie wasn't there. Thank God Gurlie isn't here, thought he, or she'd make me strike him for a raise.
> Probably all were thinking much the same thing for the moment, for there was an awkward pause. Then Mr. Wynnewood cleared his throat and resumed: Let's see the figures.

This passage suggests the following assignment: write a few paragraphs consisting of the thoughts of several people on the verge of an uncomfortable decision that involves them all. Some of the characters may decide to go ahead, others to back down. Ideally, this assignment ought to show student writers how to use mild forms of tension and release in addition to outright confrontation. Suggest to your students that if their characters have unspoken motivations, these need not be hidden—giving more information can often make writing more complex, more accurate, and I daresay more interesting. A counterexample is Ford Madox Ford's novel *The Good Soldier*, whose main character is a man who consistently fails to recognize—or acknowledge—the bad behavior of his wife and his friends. *The Good Soldier* is a good case for concealing motivations, and could possibly be taught to sophisticated high school students in tandem with *White Mule.*

•

Williams uses hidden feelings to great effect early on in the book, when Joe's sister Frieda comes to visit the newborn baby:

> Frieda's mind had wandered. She had not heard more than the first few words of what he had said. She stood at the window and dreamed children to herself. If only . . . but she would never marry now. Yes, it would have to be another girl, she thought. If it had only been mine! I would care for it, it would see the world. At night I would talk with it, teach it and it would love me. I am so lonely.

Williams gets the weight of the flat statement "I am so lonely" across because he has put a huge amount of energy behind it by shifting the voice of the paragraph from the third person to the first person, and by moving from vagueness to specificity (from Frieda's wandering to dreaming and wishing for a child), and then flatly stating the hidden feeling that caused the wish.

The writing assignment here is to choose a strong feeling (along the lines of "I am so lonely") and write a very short story or a sketch that moves from generalities to one strong feeling. Try reading Williams's paragraph backwards—doesn't it sound more like recent fiction that way? Give students the option of drafting the piece backwards—from a strong feeling to generalities—and then reversing it.

Christopher Edgar

O Pioneers!

Using In the American Grain

A daring modernist work, *In the American Grain* showcases William Carlos Williams's great range as a writer. His strange and fascinating excursion through American history up to the time of Lincoln reminds one of James Joyce in its myriad of prose styles. While the book's polyphony can make the reader feel he or she is wrestling Proteus—narrators change and disappear, primary texts blend and merge with dense passages resembling prose poems, chapters take strange turns without notice, and everything tumbles together in the epic sweep—these challenges are also what make it so rewarding. It's no coincidence that *In the American Grain* has influenced other American experimental writers, such as Hart Crane, Charles Olson, and Susan Howe.

As an inspired experiment in historical writing, *In the American Grain* offers numerous models for any writer wanting to write on an historical topic or figure, using various perspectives and period styles. Teachers of high school and college students (in English or American studies) can use *In the American Grain* to show students how history can be reimagined. The history in Williams's book is based not on accepted "truths" but on a highly personal reinterpretation, and reexperiencing, of historical conflicts and events. In this way alone, *In the American Grain* is a curative for the dry, standard history text. (It bears mentioning, too, that Williams was decades ahead of the recent emphasis on multiculturalism; he represented the clash of cultures from all points of view.)

So what is *In the American Grain*, history or fiction, and how can one use it to teach students to write? The book's origins hold some interesting clues. In a letter to the poet Horace Gregory, Williams wrote:

> Of mixed ancestry, I felt from earliest childhood that America was the only home I could ever possibly call my own. I felt that it was expressly founded for me, personally, and that it must be my first business in life to possess it; that only by making it my own from the beginning to my own day, in detail, should I ever have a basis for knowing where I stood. I must have

a basis for orienting myself formally in the beliefs which activated me from day to day.

Nothing in the school histories interested me, so I decided as far as possible to go to whatever source material I could get at and start my valuations there: to establish myself from my own reading, in my own way, in the locality which by birthright had become my own.[1]

In 1925, Williams took a sabbatical from medicine, and he and his wife Flossie rented an apartment in New York City. The couple spent many of their days doing research for *In the American Grain* in the American History room of the New York Public Library, becoming so obsessed with the task that their finely laid plans for socializing with the Manhattan literary set flew out the window. Flossie played an integral role in the project:

Mrs. Williams helped me a lot with my reading. She would sometimes dig up the material, read it and tell me about it. I always like to get things that way. In college I got quite as much from lectures as from books and always remembered more vividly what I heard than what I read. Anyhow, she did all the reading for the Aaron Burr chapter and it was, besides, her enthusiasm which fired it and which I took over complete, my part being merely to decide on the form of the make-up and go ahead.[2]

The fact that Williams would write from what Flossie *related* to him is significant, because as a method it neatly dovetailed with his notion of history as something plastic, material there to be used, and as something organic, always being reinvented and personalized. The catch is that this entailed contacting the historical actors themselves, *through* the primary sources. The truth of the connection was what mattered; Flossie became the voice of Burr, and Williams trusted the truth of her transmission. The letter continues:

The book is as much a study in styles of writing as anything else. I tried to write each chapter in the style most germane to its sources or at least the style which seemed to me appropriate to the material. To this end, where possible, I copied and used the original writings, as in the Cotton Mather chapter, the Benjamin Franklin chapter and the [John] Paul Jones chapter, of which no word is my own. I did this with malice aforethought to prove the truth of the book, since the originals fitted into it without effort on my part, perfectly, leaving not a seam.[3]

This somewhat radical attitude towards history—and writing—is also reflected in Williams's comment about Hart Crane's use of a passage from *In the American Grain* in Crane's poem sequence *The Bridge**: "[Crane] took what he wanted, why shouldn't he—that's what writing is for."[4] The fact that Williams so freely mixes primary source (found) material with his own writing can be perplexing for the reader, but at the same time it demonstrates Williams's appreciation of good historiography. Why say anything more when the primary documents say exactly what you want to say?

Historical "fact" in *In the American Grain* is made still more elusive by Williams's project of identifying the sources of an indigenous American character, as something distinct from European influences. Always a great advocate of American literature and all things American, Williams was never more impassioned on the subject. In his essay "The American Background," Williams makes an analogy that could also apply to the driving idea of *In the American Grain*:

> [The first immigrants] saw birds with rusty breasts and called them robins. Thus, from the start, an America of which they could have had no inkling drove the first settlers upon their past. They retreated for warmth and reassurance to something previously familiar. But at a cost. For what they saw were not robins. They were thrushes only vaguely resembling the rosy, daintier English bird. Larger, stronger, and in the evening of a wilder, lovelier song, actually here was something the newcomers had never in their lives before encountered.[5]

To Williams, of course, this shortsightedness is anathema. Everywhere in *In the American Grain,* he is looking for historical figures who made a leap of faith and imagination by embracing the New World and allowing it to change their thinking. Williams is interested in those pioneers who created new terms for a New World. He also wants to find what makes each of his historical figures uniquely American. Like a geologist examining stones for traces of a newly discovered mineral, Williams holds each specimen up to the light and turns it around. Sometimes he finds such traces and examines them minutely; sometimes, finding little evidence, he puts the stone in question down and moves on to the next one. Yet paradoxically—and maddeningly for the reader—Williams is

---

* I believe the passage Crane used was ironically something Williams himself had quoted directly.

anything but scientific. The originator of "no ideas but in things" seems to reverse his own credo, at times seeing individual trees only as forest: the idea takes over.

A natural focus of Williams's obsession with American uniqueness is contact between natives and colonists. Williams often interprets this contact literally, as physical contact—touch. He admires those colonists who actually lived with the natives, such as Daniel Boone, Père Sebastian Rasles, and Sam Houston. According to Williams, these men learned, through coming to understand Native American customs, how to live "close to the land" rather than huddling together on the Eastern coast, looking to Europe as the Pilgrims did.

Two chapters are especially interesting in this regard: "Père Sebastian Rasles" and "The May-Pole at Merry Mount." The Rasles chapter involves a conversation over lunch in Paris between Williams and the French poet and cosmopolitan Valery Larbaud. In this book-within-a-book, Larbaud listens patiently through Williams's long rant against Puritanism, then asks Williams about the customs and lives of the native tribes. Excited, Williams goes into much detail describing the Abnaki of Maine, who lived between the French Jesuits to the north and the Puritans to the south, and the French priest (Rasles) who comes to live with the tribe. Rasles may be Williams's single favorite character in the whole book, the one Williams is searching for, because Rasles comes to see the world from the natives' point of view. To Williams, Rasles represents "a spirit, rich, blossoming, generous, able to give and receive, full of taste, a nose, a tongue, a laugh, enduring, self-forgetful in beneficence—a new spirit in the New World. . . . He was a great MAN." Williams also writes, significantly, that Rasles lived thirty-four years with "his beloved [natives] . . . TOUCHING them every day."

In "The May-Pole at Merry Mount," Williams relates an historical event in a more straightforward narrative based on Thomas Morton's *The New English Canaan*. Morton, a New Englander with an "inclination to boisterous revelry," invites the local natives to join him and his friends in a "gambol on the green." Scandalized by the drinking and "lasciviousness" that goes on, the Puritans respond with "fantastic violence." Morton's lands are confiscated, he is put in stocks, then sent back to England for trial. What befalls the natives is left unsaid, but the message is clear: for the Puritans, social (not to mention intimate) contact with the natives is strictly forbidden, and extremely dangerous.

The amount of bloodshed in *In the American Grain* is horrific, and Williams does not shrink from recognizing the genocide that took place. The first half of the book reads like a study of spreading violence, not unlike an American *Macbeth*. The first chapter ("Red Eric") begins with a murder, and the specter of rape and killing looms over each succeeding act. Usually matter-of-fact about the violence, at other times Williams becomes quite angry. In his impassioned moments he sees the true villains as the Puritans of Massachusetts. "Trustless of humane experience, not knowing what to think, they went mad, lost all direction," he writes in his account of the Morton affair. In Williams's mind, the Puritans carried a poisonous seed to the New World and became the worst perpetrators of the religious violence that ensued. At several points Williams brings up their persecution of the Quakers, and the chapter following "The May-Pole at Merry Mount," "Cotton Mather's Wonders," is a chilling portrayal of the ultimate stage of paranoia and madness: the witch trials, the Puritans' killing of their own.

While justified on many counts, Williams's anger towards the Puritans drives him to some strange and extreme conclusions, at times skewing the book. For instance, at one point he becomes almost forgiving towards the conquistadors in his implication that, unlike the Puritans, the conquistadors' violence tied them to the New World. "No, we are not Indians but we are men of their world," says Ponce de Leon. "The blood means nothing; the spirit, the ghost of the land moves in the blood, moves the blood."[6] There is also a mystical sexual dynamic between the Europeans and the natives that Williams focuses upon, which is fascinating but at times hard to take—see, for instance, the submissive Montezuma in "The Destruction of Tenochtitlan," the "She" of the De Soto chapter, and the entire "Jacataqua" chapter. The themes that Williams probes may give some readers pause, perhaps due to their provocative nature, perhaps due to the truths underlying them. As an American, one feels as if one's own past is on the analyst's couch. But Williams's is too, of course, and you can't help but appreciate his boldness and honesty, even when you feel he goes a little too far.

In the American Grain can be read for its insights into the American past, for its radical approach to history, or for its fascination as a vessel piloted by an *idée fixe* (the American character). You can also read the book as an exercise in prose styles. When Williams becomes bullheaded and charges off in a certain direction, you have little choice except to go where he takes you, but if you suspend judgment and hang on, it's an exhilarating ride. The book's many facets also make it wonderful to reread—from a different angle or to discover new angles. Needless to say, these many facets can also inspire great class discussions.

•

Here are a few writing ideas for advanced high school and older students to try, based on individual chapters of *In the American Grain*. (Some of these assignments are fairly challenging, so feel free to adapt or simplify them.)

"Red Eric." Write a "saga," spanning several generations, in which the speaker never reveals his or her identity. Try to focus on a single conflict or event in each generation, and leave the "connections" out. "Red Eric" was based on a translation from Norse, and Williams chose a style he deliberately tried to make "barbaric and primitive." You might also try your hand at creating your own primitive style, by avoiding adjectives, adverbs, and Latinate words, and using short (perhaps one-word) sentences.

"The Discovery of the Indies." Williams later wrote about his Columbus chapter, "I had managed after all kinds of rewriting to tell about the three voyages and at the same time to keep the discovery that occurred in the first voyage for a dramatic ending. It meant turning everything around, ending with the beginning."[7] Try writing your own narrative of a significant discovery, in which events subsequent to that discovery come before the actual discovery, which comes last. (The discovery could be an early explorer's first sight of land, Edison and the light bulb, or any other.) You might try building up the tension, as Williams does, by making the narrative episodic (e.g., entries in a diary or ship's log).

"The Destruction of Tenochtitlan." Create a portrait of an extinct civilization by describing only what is left behind: records, art objects, architecture. Choose a few of these relics and from them try to piece together that civilization's customs. Or try describing a city in the New World from the eyes of a European seeing it for the first time. Imagine you are one of Cortés's men, say, walking through Tenochtitlan. What would you see? Then describe what a European might look like, at first sight, to a native of the New World. "The Tenochtitlan chapter was written in

big square paragraphs like Inca masonry. I admired the massive walls of fitted masonry—no plaster—just fitted boulders. I took that to be a wonderful example of what I wanted to do with my prose; no patchwork," Williams wrote.[8] If you want to try something really challenging, invent your own prose style derived from architecture.

"The Fountain of Eternal Youth" and "De Soto and the New World." Williams never reveals who "She" is in the De Soto chapter. Is "She" a muse, a foe, the voice of the Florida Indians, or the voice of the New World? Invent a character who speaks for one nation or tribe in conflict with another (such as a Native American tribe and a band of European colonists, or any other two nations or ethnic groups). Then create a dialogue between the two, following Williams's model: a narrative account by the one, interjected by the dramatic voice of the other.

"Sir Walter Raleigh." Write an elegy to a public figure, exalting him or her as fully as you can. Be rhapsodic—use a lot of exclamation marks and O's. You might address your elegy to an imaginary muse, as Williams does in his Raleigh chapter. (Repeating the refrain "Sing O Muse . . . " can help spur you on.)

"Cotton Mather's Wonders." This chapter is taken verbatim from the primary sources. Imagine you are a witness at the witch trials, and invent testimony exposing the Devil's work. Make your account as surreal and outlandish as you can. Note how the use of italics, small capitals, and capitalized nouns adds to the Biblical, fire-and-brimstone feel of Mather's writing. (Williams seems to have especially appreciated the effect of putting select nouns in small capitals; he continues to use small caps in subsequent chapters, and they lend a very odd emphasis to what he is saying.) Experimenting with these stylistic effects, familiar from such documents as the Bill of Rights, can be quite fun.

"George Washington." Write about the inner life of a popular figure. Fame cloaks famous people so that we see only their clothes. Take those clothes off. What is left? Does fame or a sense of duty cause popular figures to create different personae? How does Washington feel when he can finally retire to Mount Vernon? Is there someone inside dying to get out? Williams also wrote a libretto called "The First President" (in *Many Lives and Other Plays*). You can write about these inner lives in dramatic

monologues, or use a medley of styles (e.g., combine poems, prose, and playscripts).

Another approach is to portray an historical figure *just before* a pivotal moment (e.g., Custer on the morning of Little Big Horn, or Truman deciding whether or not to drop the bomb). Pretend you are a camera, capturing the visual details of the scene. Then go inside the figure's mind—what are his or her secret thoughts?

"Abraham Lincoln." Or try the opposite: take an historical figure and make him or her larger than life, iconic. Williams's Lincoln is like an omniscient spirit, a guardian angel touching many lives in many eras. Write a piece that is a series of examples of this spirit touching individual lives.

Finally, here are two more general writing ideas:

1) Imagine you are having a conversation about American history with someone, possibly a foreigner. You can say anything you want. Improvise. See where this takes you.

2) Write about an historical event, figure, or epoch from the point of view of someone who "knows everything" about that subject and is holding forth, perhaps arrogantly or even wrongly. Don't be afraid to bend the facts to support your manias.

For more ideas about combining American history—or any history—with imaginative writing, see Margot Fortunato Galt's *The Story in History: Writing Your Way into the American Experience* (Teachers & Writers Collaborative, 1992).

Notes

1. William Carlos Williams, *The Selected Letters of William Carlos Williams*, p. 185.

2. Ibid., p. 186.

3. Ibid., p. 187.

4. William Carlos Williams, *I Wanted to Write a Poem*, p. 43.

5. William Carlos Williams, *Selected Essays*, p. 134.

6. William Carlos Williams, *In the American Grain*, p. 39.

7. *I Wanted to Write a Poem*, p. 42.

8. Ibid., pp. 42–43.

Bibliography

Williams, William Carlos. *The Autobiography of William Carlos Williams*. New York: New Directions, 1967.

———. *In the American Grain*. New York: New Directions, 1956.

———. *I Wanted to Write a Poem: The Autobiography of the Works of a Poet*. Reported and edited by Edith Heal. New York: New Directions, 1978.

———. *Selected Essays*. New York: New Directions, 1969.

———. *The Selected Letters of William Carlos Williams*. John C. Thirlwall, ed. New York: New Directions, 1984.

Penny Harter

Beautiful Thing

Discovering Paterson

William Carlos Williams's epic poem *Paterson*, along with books by two other authors, had been assigned to the eleventh graders at Santa Fe Preparatory School as summer reading, but after vacation, many of the students admitted that they still hadn't read *Paterson*. I had to admit to myself that I sympathized with them. Over the years, I had read almost all of Williams's other poems and a number of his short stories and essays, but, like my students, I had been intimidated by *Paterson*'s length and texture.

Paterson is a complex work involving several different types of verse, passages of prose seemingly lifted from other sources, varying kinds of dialogue, and shifting levels of diction, geographically grounded in the city of Paterson, New Jersey, and the surrounding region, from prehistory to the 1950s. However, the presentation is hardly chronological; in Book IV, Part II, a Cold War tract on money and a letter from Allen Ginsberg precede Part III's newspaper clipping from the 1850s. *Paterson* features a cast of real and imagined characters. At times it reads like a play; at others, a philosophical tract. The theme of relationships recurs throughout—person to person, person to place, person to culture, and the poet to all of these and to the language itself.

Appendices in our edition[1] include almost seventy pages of notes, rather daunting for secondary school students. To provide a frame of reference for *Paterson* and to summarize its major themes, my husband Bill, who has many close connections with the book and with the city itself, had prepared a handout (appended to this essay).

Over the summer, I finally did read *Paterson*, still not fully engaging with it, although I found passages that intrigued me. I think the later experience of reading and hearing large sections out loud in class helped me to catch fire with the work and communicate my growing enthusiasm. At first, my students were reluctant to read orally, so I did most of it. But as we became aware of the cadences of Williams's lines, the overlapping and building themes, the random yet inevitable progression of images, more students dared to read out loud. One student insisted on reading certain passages, the ones with the Marcia Nardi letters, and she delighted in taking on the persona of Nardi. Others wanted to read the historical and journalistic excerpts.

My small class of ten students represented a wide range of abilities. Most of them had attended Prep from seventh through tenth grades, so they had done the challenging reading and writing the school requires, and they were used to discussing and responding to literature both creatively and analytically. A few, recent transfer students unaccustomed to such rigor, had more trouble engaging with the work. Although this suggests that taking on the whole book should be reserved for a more advanced class, one could use portions of *Paterson* with any average eleventh or twelfth grade group.

Paterson consists of five "books," and we went through them, book by book, recognizing the major themes and answering the questions raised in Bill's handout. We did not read aloud or discuss every page; sometimes I skipped several pages, because of time limits (we had ten fifty-minute class periods for *Paterson*) and because I sensed that the class would be more (or less) interested in certain passages. Also I encouraged students to look over the excellent notes in our edition.

We talked about the techniques—in addition to collage—Williams used in *Paterson*, and all the students absorbed at least some of his methods, as demonstrated in the long poems they eventually wrote. At the least, they became comfortable with irregular verse lines, and most of them developed a freedom of movement on the page similar to the variety of line Williams employs. For example, Book II, Part III opens with very short couplets, moves quickly past a much longer couplet into the triadic line he was experimenting with at the time, then goes back into a left-margin anchored free verse with irregular stanzas, and so on.

Students learned to move freely among present reality, recollection, fantasy, and more meditative passages, creating a collage texture in both content and form, as Williams does. At the same time, many students developed words or phrases into refrains that recur in their poems, like Williams's "So be it" that takes on a mantric quality early in Book III, Part I, or the exclamation "Beautiful thing!" that turns up at odd moments throughout *Paterson* and reminds readers of the search for beauty that pervades the whole work.

Several students also delighted in seeking out language not usually acknowledged as legitimate in the classroom—such as the special argots of teen hangouts, computer games, new-age culture, advertising, and the like—embedding phrases or page-long examples, often versified, into the body of their works. These resembled Williams's inclusions of private speech, dialect, and letters in *Paterson*, and, as with Williams, these were sometimes fabrications and sometimes verbatim transcripts.

Other inclusions à la Williams were paragraphs lifted from historical documents describing the landscape and people of a given time and place, snippets from newspapers, and quotations from greater or lesser historical figures or from popular books, artfully juxtaposed with current images or events from the students' own experience. As one might expect, a number of students included reflections of video culture, ranging from transcripts of newscasts to descriptions of on-screen visuals. One student even included several photographs she had taken of the environment in which her poem was set, at one point layering lines of verse at odd angles over a photo so that the words interacted with its visual content.

In effect, for these students, reading *Paterson* became an extension of the natural process of learning their native language. They found themselves freed to move at will across and down the page, to include what seemed appropriate with or without logical connections, to express multiple realities in the span of a page. For most of them, these freedoms became natural and fluid. I doubt that the students will ever view poetry in quite the same way as they did before encountering *Paterson*.

At the end of the unit, the class and I were both proud that we had "gotten through" *Paterson*. It turned out that the other eleventh grade teacher had begun it but found that his class wasn't interested in continuing; he preferred the other two summer reading assignments—a novel and a memoir—perhaps because he himself writes fiction. But on the last day with *Paterson* in our class, all my students agreed that discovering *Paterson* had indeed been a "beautiful thing."

A First Creative Response

As we were just beginning book III, I handed out several pages of quotations from *Paterson* and asked the students to write spontaneously in class whatever came to them in response to the quotations they selected.

Some of their responses became short, independent pieces; others ended up in their later, longer works. Here is one of Victoria Tishman's short responses (the Williams quotation is in italics):

> *and I am aware of the stream*
> *that has no language, coursing*
> *beneath the quiet heaven of*
> *your eyes*
>
> I am aware of the person who
> needs no face and features—
> will always be unchangeable
>
> as I am aware of the invisible beauty
> you know, but choose not to recognize,
> in me
>
> finally, I am aware of the real you
> NOT your superficial beauty
>> but the real you
>> the inner strength
>> makes your outer
> fake
>> beauty true

Students were eager to share their short pieces, and their success fueled their desire to attempt longer works. In the short pieces, they showed that they were absorbing Williams's concerns and style, and something of his confidence.

Their Own "Patersons"

When we had finished Book IV, I asked the students each to write a "Book" of their own that, in some way, echoed Williams's methods, themes, and style. Each piece had to be six to ten pages long (regular font, double-spaced). They were to focus on a place they knew well, either current or remembered, and include historical records, news clippings, and letters, as well as asides to themselves and descriptions of persons and landscapes in their own voices. If they wished, they could include their earlier short pieces, or build the longer work around one of them. They were given a week to work on this at home, with a day for hearing and rereading each other's drafts midway through the week.

As we began Book V, I brought in related materials, including Allen Ginsberg's poem "Sunflower Sutra," poems of Sappho, and two books with art works that Williams refers to: Brueghel's *Nativity* and the unicorn tapestries at The Cloisters. The Brueghel picture led to a discussion of why Williams liked Brueghel's work, and how Brueghel echoed Williams's credo "No ideas but in things."

The day their Books were due, everyone in the class was eager to share what they had written. We applauded each effort, noting both how it was similar to Williams and how it differed. The students' writing was wonderful. Because of space limitations, I can quote excerpts from only two of them:

Sitting Naked, Now, in a Place Called Bedgerume. Naked.
(*excerpts*)

by Callie Silver

white carpet on pale bottom and toenails wide neglected.
—Sorry, honey, but I suspected that you
—I can't cry anymore!

She then sent her kittens out to play in the garden and warned them to keep their clothes neat and clean. This, of course, was useless, for as soon as they were out of sight, the three kittens began to run around and climb on the rocks. Tom Kitten got his clothes caught and torn in the bushes and lost his hat. And the girls managed to lose their pinafores, too.[2]

So, bad kitty, sad kitty, mad kitty, glad kitty, 'ad a kitty
fo' suppah. Took a pen knahf and 'ad to dig, raght, 'cause the skin
were real tough, but I tore it off and my 'ands was soaked through
Ah mean to the bone (the kitty's) and did ya know a kitty's innahds
is stringy-like? but we roasted her up and found us some wild mushrooms and had ourselves a reg'lah feast! Had a kitty fo' mah suppah.

[. . .]

Cannot sleep
   Should try sleep
      —oft' to weep—
        off to weep.
Sitting in a place called bedge rume.

Anyways, I like Picasso's blue period and thought of you. PS—I'm
kinda worried that I got food poisoning. I ate this gyro that was
being prepared by this woman w/out gloves who was also handling
money. . . . you like blue . . .[3]

Sitting, now, naked, still. painting The walls a creamy sky baby
ocean cornflower Copenhagen blue. Took days to paint
     —don't let puppy step in that pan! Ah, the memories of the oldens.

     [. . .]

She leaned her head back so that a 45 degree angle was formed in
the crook of her neck. She inhaled oxygen and exhaled carbon diox-
ide, through each lung chamber and touching each blood cell. Her
nostrils flared to concave in form, her eyebrows semi-circles of tis-
sue. Her knees contracted, retracted, attracted, extracted, protracted.
(And that was that. (For now.))
Three .wood.hearts ..
Hang .on.wall ..
See .them.there ..
Look .right.there ..
Red .on.blue ..
Hearts .wood.three ..

                    You can be swaying in . . in No Time! your
introductory lesson is FREE. So call today and start having more
fun.[4]

     Are you having a good time? Who is your rival this year? Is
there new face . . . ?[5]

leaning back on elbows now
shut—eyes stretch—legs stretch—neck breathe breathe
extend—elbow tighten—belly lower—bottom breathe breathe
inhale—totally exhale—totally remember—justtobe
every now and then (all for now)

     [. . .]

stretch out the arms and form a perfect white and black form, a
stepped-on oval (), hear the bones in the shoulders crack, then the
funny bone laughs so hard it turns to dust and floats away in the
wind of a wine-scented belch, a whole-hearted belly laugh
taste your tears and eat the bitters because you are what you are
'cause they are your people, see what they endured for you, feel their
sorrow at being enslaved and being ripped out of their
homeland, their mother country

→→→→the walls are still blue and you are still naked—these things
you can count on!

Saturday, September 18, 1965
261st day—104 days to come
        La da de da. I love that beautiful music. And I don't care if I
have lots of packing to do. Elliot's car wouldn't start last night. Tuff.
The game was lots of fun (score 20-20). And who did we see but
Michelle Simon? Small world. The Minnesota Gophers. Chuckle.
Guess we'll be going to Flo's tonight. Wonder what the present is.
And to the big drawing in Hollywood. Hope we get more![6]

She wrote that sixteen years before the birth of her daughter.
She wrote the entry in the blue ink from a ball point pen.
These these these these these! things you can count on:
blue paint, red hearts,

        the silence of close friendship
        swim meets
        home, where we tie one end
                of the thread of life
            knit tights
making love on a secluded
                beach
velvet-starred nights
rolling up your sleeves
the first drops of rain on the
                roof
the dew, the air, the sounds
                of the birds
wild blueberries blanketing
                coastal Maine[7]

        Picture it.
Your index finger cracks off because it is too cold. Your tongue is
furry and numb. A trail of fiery blood soaks into the snow. Your
teeth are rotting out of your mouth. You hiccup with stomach pain,
hot metal rods of pain poking your intestines and the back of your
throat. Is there no savior? you ask. But first you ask, Where might I
find a piece of bread?
        Picture it.
the following things are those which
you

can
count on :-)

                    seeing objects formed by clouds
when your ship comes in
                    the fogging of bathroom mirrors
fishing for compliments
                    putting trouble into a boat of leaves and sailing it out
                    to sea
counting your blessings
                    beach-side yoga
blue-banded white pottery[8]

These   the   you   count
        are   things   can   on

while naked in a blue-painted room.

                              •

Galisteo (*excerpt*)

by Chris Holloway

                    Ruins dissolving back to earth,
                              vultures lurking in a dead tree.
empty playground swings blowing in the breeze.
                    Images of ghost children
                              dust rising up from the barefoot children
the wind whistling through ancient graveyards.
                    mud growing as the rain falls,
                              farolitos burning on a cold winter night
lighting the way to the church.
                    piñons dressed in their once a year lights,
                              endless descriptions.

From anywhere in the village of Galisteo, either once or twice a day, the one whistle of the train can be heard. Unlike other small towns where the train goes directly through the town and is the main attraction, Galisteo is just the opposite. The train ventures through the outskirts of the town, although its presence is not, and will never be, forgotten. Don't get me wrong; it's not the type of situation where the train comes so close that the midnight shift wakes you up at three forty-five each and every morning. In cases such as this the whistle of the passing train can be quite annoying.

On the contrary, the train that moves through the outskirts of Galisteo is as peaceful as the wind. Each time I hear that distinct howl (as in what dogs do) of the train, it makes me wonder where it's headed and where it's coming from. Someday I'll figure it out, but for now I will just use my imagination. So be it! So be it!

> The creek swells as the rain
> continues to fall.
> Larger rocks begin to roll.
> As the water rushes ever faster,
> a fence post gives way.
> A cow skull floats by.
> Dry land is overtaken
> by the tons of rushing water.

An American soldier described his impressions of the village in 1846: "Visited Galisteo, which contains about 200 inhabitants. The houses are built of adobe, or sun-dried bricks, whitewashed inside, and with flat roofs, as in Bible times. . . . The waters in the mountains converge into streams and fertilize a depression in the valley, so that corn can be raised sufficient for the scanty dish of atole and tortillas used by the people. Some wheat is also raised; threshed by hand, winnowed by the breath, or by throwing in the air, ground between two stones by the women, and baked into very tolerable bread—for hungry men. The cooking utensils are pots and bowls of earthenware made by the Pueblo Indians . . . A kind of incipient cheese, or curds compressed by hand, is made in profusion, and is no doubt wholesome. The inhabitants at this season rarely sleep in their houses, but spread their mats or blankets before their doors and sleep in the open air. In daytime, their beds are folded up and used for seats inside the rooms. The kitchens have neat chimneys in the corners . . . several looms are seen . . . also spinning wheels of rude construction. The village has a church, about thirty feet long and twenty feet wide, neatly whitewashed inside . . .

"Visited Galisteo this afternoon and had some further insight into the characters and habits of the villagers. The people are rather filthy in their cooking and their persons . . . this is true of the lower orders, the great mass of the people. The arrival of Senor Pino, the owner of the village, reported, and fandango spoken of for the evening."[9]

> The things represent, toenails,
> beer cans, telephones,
> cats, grass,
> mailboxes, fire,
> snow, gravel,
> paper, burnt-out light bulbs,

> compost, weedeater,
> power, death,
> potsherds, raccoon shit,
> kevlar, garlic.
> WHAT GIVES?

The Galisteo creek always has a certain peace and quiet to it. No matter what time of day the creek is visited, it is always different. Not considerably different, but a new sound or creature can be heard. The creek bed is clustered with hundreds of cottonwood trees and Russian olive trees. Each leaf on these towering trees can also be heard, when the crisp and nearly constant breeze is blowing. Each drop of water and brushing of weeds can be heard if only concentrated upon. The creek, in a way, is the main vein of Galisteo. In a certain way the creek brings joy to the town. In the spring the cottonwoods are full with life in their bright green color while in the fall their luminescent yellowish-orange leaves leave us with a smile for winter.

Closure and Other Possibilities

We finished our study of *Paterson* with an animated discussion of the following questions that I brought in, and some further questions the students wanted to address. Questions 1–10 are mine (with some help from Bill), and 11–20 are theirs.

Discussion Questions

1) Why might Williams choose to end with a focus on the tapestries? How would the mood have been different if he'd ended with Book IV?
2) How does the hunt for the unicorn echo one of Williams's main themes? Does the outcome differ?
3) How does the whole of Book V compare with the tapestries?
4) What is Williams's relationship with the landscape? The city?
5) List dominant themes throughout the book.
6) List dominant symbols throughout the book.
7) How does this poem differ from other poems you've read?
8) What is delicate about Williams's poetry? What is coarse and harsh?
9) Why do you think he chose to write about Paterson instead of New York City?

10) What is his relationship to the text? What is he trying to do? Is he writing for others to read or for himself?
11) What is the link between the nativity and the unicorn?
12) How would this whole work be different if it had been written by a woman?
13) Is Williams dispassionate in his writing?
14) Is his writing "selfish" or "personal"? What is the difference between the two?
15) Discuss how his opinion of beauty includes vulgarity. Do you agree?
16) Is he justified in using a collage style in *Paterson*, and what effect does he produce by doing so?
17) Discuss Williams's attitudes toward women with examples from the text.
18) Is William Carlos Williams "cool"?
19) What are Williams's feelings toward a classical versus an idiomatic style?
20) Why did he write the book? Does it end?

With more time or a different orientation I might have pursued other kinds of assignments or methods. For example, a few students did some historical research; had I emphasized this angle more strongly, it could have led to collaborations with their history teachers, and perhaps some oral history work with parents and grandparents and other elders.

With larger classes, one could form groups of four to six students, with each group working on an aspect of their actual city, to make up one Book. With the results collected into one work, the whole class could discuss possible revisions and ways to emphasize common themes.

Whatever focus might become prominent in students' discussion and work related to *Paterson*, I would want them to experience the primary features of collage, by including much that they wrote themselves (and a diversity of formal approaches to modern verse in that writing) and a sense of the continuing presence of historical events and figures in their own lives. Coming to terms with *Paterson* will then help students in their own struggles to find identity and beauty in their lives and the world around them.

Appendix: Preliminary Handout for a Study of Paterson

Notice: This handout (copyright © 1997 William J. Higginson) may be reproduced without permission by individual teachers for classroom use in the study of Paterson. *For any other use, contact Teachers & Writers Collaborative.*

INTRODUCTION TO WILLIAM CARLOS WILLIAMS'S *PATERSON*

by William J. Higginson

> *An epic is a poem containing history.*—Ezra Pound

You have read some of Homer, made a sort of beginning on the epic, the story of a hero. But by the twentieth century things changed. Ezra Pound put history into one of the longest poems of his generation, *The Cantos*, grabbing everything from bits of old Chinese classics to parts of World War II he witnessed himself.

Pound's college buddy, William Carlos Williams, became a doctor (obstetrics and pediatrics) as well as a poet. He knew life with a scalpel, a splint, a bandage. It was not all pretty, not all "historic" (in the sense of important to the course of human history), but all real. WCW wanted to get life, and language, raw, into his work. While Pound and T. S. Eliot abandoned America for Europe, WCW searched for "the American idiom," listening to the speech of people in his office in Rutherford, N.J, his hospital in Passaic, and his beloved Paterson, city of vaudeville (Lou Costello was from Paterson), of labor unions and cops, and of factories for locomotives and silk, as well as the location of one of the great natural wonders of America, the Passaic Falls, right in the middle of the city—and in New York's Greenwich Village, where he socialized with artists and writers when he could get away from doctoring.

He wrote many of his early poems quickly on prescription blanks and any other scraps he could get his hands on, so they were often short, with short lines. You may have seen "The Red Wheelbarrow" and other brief early poems. But he wanted to stretch out, and though it took him years to get at it the way he wanted to, he succeeded in *Paterson*, and in a number of other later poems.

What is unique about *Paterson*? Williams threw in anything that seemed relevant. There are letters from Allen Ginsberg—then a beginning poet who had lived in Paterson—and others, some unknown. There's an inventory of the estate of a man who died in 1803. And while Pound was forever quoting Latin and Chinese philosophers and sometimes poets—male—WCW made one of the best translations ever done of a poem by Sappho (a Greek woman), in Book V, part II, the first sixteen lines of verse.

More important, while working on *Paterson*, Williams finally achieved a method for recording the rhythms of American speech in verse, his famous triadic line. The first, and one of the greatest, illustrations of this is in the famous section that he also made a free-standing poem entitled "The Descent"; in *Paterson* it's near the beginning of Book II, part III, beginning with the lines "The descent beckons / as the ascent beckoned / Memory is a kind" on through the line "endless and indestructible   ." (Yes, in the original the extra space is there before the period; WCW didn't always do the expected with punctuation.)

Each Book of *Paterson* is a unit; certain themes run through all. Water, the river. Money, the American dream. The titles of the Books are significant. Prose passages are usually quoted from letters, newspapers, documents. Don't expect a simple construction. Some things to watch for:

Book I. Preface. "Rigor of beauty is the quest." Yes, WCW is looking for beauty. But not the easy beauty of traditional art. Like a dog, he goes around sniffing everything, looking for it. Part I. We are introduced to the "man" Paterson, sleeping as part of the landscape. The man, the city, the landscape, are all one. Paradoxically, the man travels around the city (that is himself). And he has a history. A further confusion: His middle name, "Faitoute" (French: "does everything"), is also an alias for an acquaintance of WCW's in real life, who gets into the poem by providing some of the materials the poet's forever putting into it. Most important, here WCW first says "no ideas but in things"—and repeats it. It's his manifesto, his creed that he found while writing this poem. What does it mean? *Part II.* Why is divorce "the sign of knowledge in our time"? (Remember, when he was writing, divorce from marriage was much less common than it is today. Other kinds of "divorce"?) "Carlos" is the uncle from whom he gets his middle name—one he's very proud of; Uncle Carlos was a doctor. *Part III.* The quotation from Symonds at the end of Book I might be a summation of some of WCW's ideas, not in specifics, but in general. He quotes it at least to show that others before him have worked at ways to mirror a real world rather than just create a pretty ideal. (The difficult word *choliambi* is a transliteration of one of the Greek terms two lines above; pronounce it "*ko*-lee-*am*-bee.")

Book II. Parts I and II. What and who are "Americans"? What is "the American dream"? Alexander Hamilton was a founder of Paterson, hoped to make a lot of money from it, as well as see it help build the economy of the young nation. (See my comments about him at the end of this sheet.)

Book III. Part I. Williams disliked libraries, wanted to be out in the world gathering fresh sensations. But the library yields the secrets of the past. "Beautiful thing!" Is he getting closer? To what? *Part II.* A great fire destroyed most of downtown Paterson, including the library, in 1902; so much money was available that the city was almost entirely rebuilt within a year. Beautiful thing? Note early mention of tapestry (it dominates Book V). *Part III.* Writing, how to? Experiments with collage, dialect (read it out loud to figure out the sense), the list (well driller's findings), critiques, and songs.

Book IV. Part I. Corydon and Phyllis, a wealthy woman and her nurse. Note the innuendo and manipulation in their relationship. And Phyllis's with others, including Paterson (him again?). *Part II.* Note the atomic age has come in, and into the poem. Longish letter from "A.G." (Allen Ginsberg). Money, credit. (See my note at end of this sheet.) American dream theme. *Part III.* Language again. Another Ginsberg letter. Child abuse, murder, death. WCW originally intended to end *Paterson* here. Why didn't he?

Book V. This book, now that Paterson (the man? the book? the author?) has made it to the sea in Book IV, can go beyond the city of Paterson, and it does. The tapestries (and the themes WCW sees in them) are at The Cloisters, a museum near the Hudson River on New York City's Upper West Side. The museum building is a reconstruction of parts of a medieval monastery, and houses a group of tapestries, depicting various stages of the hunt for a unicorn, beautifully shown as looking like a young white horse, with its one horn sticking two feet or so straight out of its forehead. Some truly great verse here, in WCW's invented mode. *Part II.* Ginsberg letter, artists. Note the interview and critique of an earlier WCW poem at end of Part II. *Part III.* Art, flowers, verse. Is this ending finally a true ending?

Evidently, Williams wanted the poem to go on. But there is no real Book VI, just bits and pieces that might have fit in, if he hadn't died first. Did you feel as though it was over at the end of Book IV? Of Book V?

NOTE: *As with any work "containing history," Paterson is full of names of people and places unfamiliar to most readers. Usually you don't need to know more about them than what appears in the text to understand what's going on. There will also be words that you may not know. Use a good dictionary or a one-volume desk encyclopedia. There is one historical character you should know about, Alexander Hamilton (1755–1804), who fought in the American Revolution, supported the Constitution, and was the first Secretary of the Treasury. He helped found the Society for Establishing Useful Manufactures, which first developed the area of the Passaic Falls into an industrial complex that soon became the City of Paterson. He was killed by Aaron Burr in a duel at Weehawken, New Jersey. Usury means lending money at interest, especially high interest (anything above 3%); Social Credit was a popular plan to put more money in the hands of the common people, to give them "purchasing power" and thus get the American economy out of the Great Depression in the 1930s.*

Notes

1. William Carlos Williams. *Paterson.* Revised edition prepared by Christopher MacGowan (New York: New Directions, 1995).

2. From *The Story of Tom Kitten* by Beatrix Potter.

3. Postcard from Amanda.

4. Newspaper advertisement for ballroom dancing classes.

5. From a letter from Etsuko.

6. Entry from Leda's diary.

7. Some of the "blue things" from *14,000 Things to Be Happy About* by Barbara Ann Kipfer.

8. Some of the "blue things" from *14,000 Things to Be Happy About,* by Barbara Ann Kipfer.

9. Quoted in Christina Singleton Mednick, *San Cristobal*, Robin A. Gould, ed. (Santa Fe: Palace Press/Museum of New Mexico, 1996), p. 142.

Allen Ginsberg

An Exposition of William Carlos Williams's Poetic Practice

(This 1975 lecture was first published in *Loka 2: A Journal from The Naropa Institute*, in Boulder, Colorado, and reprinted in *Composed on the Tongue*, Bolinas, California: Grey Fox, 1980.)

William Carlos Williams was living around Paterson, in Rutherford, New Jersey, and he decided that he would try and write a monumental epic (a poem, according to Pound, which includes history). Paterson was ten miles or so away—Rutherford was a little too small, like a village, Paterson was like a small city, with city history back to the American Revolution—Alexander Hamilton founding the tax-free capitalistic Society of Useful Manufacturers, to tap the electric power coming off the great falls in Paterson, second largest waterfall in the North American continent, second only to Niagara. So there was a long history of economic manipulation, or Hamilton versus Jefferson, a major theme in American economic history, which Pound was interested in and turned Williams on to. So Williams decided to use Paterson as an epic center.

Paterson

Before the grass is out the people are out
and bare twigs still whip the wind—
when there is nothing, in the pause between
snow and grass in the parks and at the street ends
—Say it, no ideas but in things—
nothing but the blank faces of the houses
and cylindrical trees
bent, forked by preconception and accident
split, furrowed, creased, mottled, stained
secret—into the body of the light—

These are the ideas, savage and tender
somewhat of the music, et cetera
of Paterson, that great philosopher—

He's making the town into a man, a town with the unconscious of a person, "moving around inside the windows of the buses." So this is his scheme for the whole poem.

> From above, higher than the spires, higher
> even than the office towers, from oozy fields
> abandoned to grey beds of dead grass
> black sumac, withered weed stalks
> mud and thickets cluttered with dead leaves—
> the river comes pouring in above the city
> and crashes from the edge of the gorge
> in a recoil of spray and rainbow mists—
> —Say it, no ideas but in things—
> and factories crystallized from its force,
> like ice from spray upon the chimney rocks

> . . . . .

> Say it! No ideas but in things. Mr.
> Paterson has gone away
> to rest and write. Inside the bus one sees
> his thoughts sitting and standing. His thoughts
> alight and scatter—

> Who are these people (how complex
> this mathematic) among whom I see myself
> in the regularly ordered plateglass of
> his thoughts, glimmering before shoes and bicycles—?
> They walk incommunicado, the
> equation is beyond solution, yet
> its sense is clear—that they may live
> his thought is listed in the Telephone
> Directory—

> and there's young Alex Shorn
> whose dad the boot-black bought a house
> and painted it inside
> with seascapes of a pale green monochrome—
> the infant Dionysus springing from
> Apollo's arm—the floors oakgrained in
> Balkan fashion—Hermes' nose, the body
> of a gourmand, the lips of Cupid, the eyes
> the black eyes of Venus' sister—

But who! who are these people? It is
his flesh making the traffic, cranking the car
buying the meat—
Defeated in achieving the solution they
fall back among cheap pictures, furniture
filled silk, cardboard shoes, bad dentistry
windows that will not open, poisonous gin
scurvy, toothache—

    .   .   .   .   .

But never, in despair and anxiety
forget to drive wit in, in till it
discover that his thoughts are decorous and simple
and never forget that though his thoughts are decorous
and simple, the despair and anxiety

the grace and detail of
a dynamo—

Divine thought! Jacob fell backwards off the press
and broke his spine. What pathos, what mercy
of nurses (who keep birthday books)
and doctors who can't speak proper english—
is here correctly on a spotless bed
painless to the Nth power—the two legs
perfect without movement or sensation

Twice a month Paterson receives letters
from the Pope, his works are translated
into French, the clerks in the post office
ungum the rare stamps from his packages
and steal them for their children's albums

So in his high decorum he is wise

    .   .   .   .   .

What wind and sun of children stamping the snow
stamping the snow and screaming drunkenly
The actual, florid detail of cheap carpet
amazingly upon the floor and paid for
as no portrait ever was—Canary singing
and geraniums in tin cans spreading their leaves
reflecting red upon the frost—
They are the divisions and imbalances

of his whole concept, made small by pity
and desire, they are—no ideas beside the facts—

This is a little essay setting up his major conceptions for his long poem *Paterson*. And coming back over and over again and warning himself not to build any large-scale poetic system apart from facts or present "ideas" other than "facts." The reason I read this is that the repeated mysterious phrase "Say it, no ideas but in things," finally turns into his re-definition, "no ideas besides the facts," and is now put down so simply, once and for all, that by this time you must understand it. I remember the first time I heard that phrase I thought, "Now what does that mean?" Would anyone like to explain it?

STUDENT: I was thinking that it means not talking in abstract jargon, philosophy, or political explanations. Not to define people in terms of categories.

GINSBERG: If it's *not* that, what *is* it?

STUDENT: Maybe it's to relate to the local specifics that they are handling physically and mentally in the particular.

STUDENT: It's also a question of phenomenology, like when you try to sever the audience from the phenomenon, it becomes sentimentality.

GINSBERG: For those who are involved with philosophical language, I guess that Williams's practice would fall into the area of phenomenology—that is, to study the actual data of the senses.

STUDENT: There's a Zen story about a question a master asked his students. This is the graduation and he has to pass it on to one of his students and he puts a picture on the table, and one student describes the picture, the other one walks up and kicks it off, and he becomes the next master.

GINSBERG: Because he had actual contact with the object, rather than verbal. "The object is a symbol of itself" is what Chogyam Trungpa has been saying re iconography—and Ezra Pound said, "The natural object is always the adequate symbol." Which is saying the same thing as "no ideas but in things."

There are some direct instructions in *Selected Essays* (New Directions, 1969) which extend his practice out a little—background to "no ideas but in things." Everybody says "play Zen," everybody says "be grounded," but very few are able to *practice* it. Williams here has actually given you several decades of actual practice in observation and notation, so you know he's sincere, you know he's real, you know he's grounded, he knows what he is doing. If you *study* him, the generalization "no ideas but in things" makes sense. So it's really interesting to see what he has to say when he does make critical generalizations, because he knows what he's practicing. In the "Prologue to *Kora in Hell*," he suggests that if you are "sketching," you are *looking*; as you walk around in Boulder, looking at detail, how do you pick out detail from the general mass of trees, how do you describe one tree out of many trees? His phrasing for that might be "How could you find the true value of that one tree?" Because "The true value is that peculiarity which gives an object a character by itself." (*Selected Essays*, p. 11). I had at one time thought that in that sentence he had given specific directions—to pick out the aspect of a tree which makes it *different* from another tree, and then using that detail to describe the tree. But that was only my interpretation of what Williams said, so I'll claim credit for that invention, for that particular practice! If you want to describe a tree, don't try to describe every atom, and don't try to describe every leaf, or every cut and crinkle in the bark. You have to pick out that aspect of the tree, whether a broken branch or two horn-like limbs at the top that come forth above the leaves, or a cluster of caterpillars' nests in one lower branch, or the "scarlet and pink shoot-tips waving delicately in the breeze" or whatever you want. Whatever detail, whatever "particularity" of the tree that strikes your eye first, or stands out in the tree. The same is true for describing a person, a guy with a big nose with snot hanging down, you've got the whole face there. Most beginning writers have difficulty describing a specific person because they don't know where to begin. They say, well, shall I begin with the shoes, or what? You should begin with either the first grotesque thing that meets your eye or that particular detail of a person, a tree, a train, or a car which is most singular at first glance or memory. "The true value is that peculiarity which gives an object a character by itself." That's a sort of direction for how you go about picking out detail. The true value of Allen Ginsberg is that peculiar twist of mind, of voice, which gives me character by myself—like a paralyzed right cheek at the moment.

He was writing in that Prologue about the difficulty of getting people to actually look at their own local detail—because everybody wants to write some sort of "poetry," they tend to look for a gilded aspect of reality. "To me this is the gist of the whole matter. It is easy to fall under the spell of a certain mode, especially if it be remote of origin..."(*Selected Essays,* p. 11). That's sort of like Donovan's lyrics, or Kahlil Gibran. "It is easy to fall under the spell of a certain mode, especially if it be remote of origin, leaving thus certain of its members essential to a reconstruction of its significance permanently lost in an impenetrable mist of time. But the thing that always stands permanently in the way of really good writing is always one: the virtual impossibility of lifting to the imagination those things *which lie under the direct scrutiny of the senses, close to the nose.* [My italics.] It is this difficulty which sets a value upon all works of art, and makes them a necessity." So "no ideas but in things," or "close to the nose."

STUDENT: Can you observe words that way?

GINSBERG: Yes. It relates to something we were talking about before when someone asked me, "Since Williams, what's been accomplished in poetics, what new things have been added?" And we talked about Gertrude Stein's practice of building little sculptures of words. Williams does this occasionally—and he wrote quite a bit about Stein. His idea of what she was doing—and what language can do. He was bugged that the poetry of his time hadn't cleaned itself out from older associations with European language and with European form.

Incidentally, on the Americanist background, there's the long essay, "The American Background," (*Selected Essays,* p. 134)—if you want to check into what the common thinking was of all those modernist people hanging around together decades ago in New York. That will give you the main gist of it. Here are a few other piths from *Selected Essays* (pp. 289–91): "The Poem as a Field of Action":

> Now we come to the question of the origin of our discoveries. Where else can what we are seeking arise from but speech? From speech, from American speech as distinct from English speech, or presumably so, if what I say above is correct. In any case (since we have no body of poems comparable to the English) from what we *hear* in America. Not, that is, from

a study of the classics, not even the American "Classics"—the *dead* classics which—may I remind you, we have *never heard* as living speech. No one has or can *hear* them as they were written any more than we can hear Greek today.

I say this once again to emphasize what I have often said—that we here must *listen* to the language for the discoveries we hope to make. . . .

It is there, in the mouths of the living, that the language is changing and giving new means for expanded possibilities in literary expression and, I add, basic structure—the most important of all.

Thus his prescription for paying attention to actual sound, your own words coming out of your own mouth—like a doctor-scientist classifying, labeling, rearranging rhythms of your own talk, literally going back to the raw material of your own ear.

He was writing here of W. H. Auden, the British poet come to America (who Williams felt didn't quite make it, in this mode, because he still was hearing an English speech). But he was pointing out that Auden came here because he knew the vigor of the speech here as distinct from England—people were actually listening to their own talk. And he was putting down Eliot for that reason, Eliot didn't exploit that possibility.

Now, both on this theme of speech-mindfulness and on the theme of samatha meditation which begins at the end of your nose, is a 1939 introduction (*Selected Essays*, pp. 233–34) to the assembled works and paintings of Charles Sheeler:

> To be an artist, as to be a good artisan, a man must know his materials. But in addition he must possess that really glandular perception of their uniqueness which realizes in them an end in itself, each piece irreplaceable by a substitute, not to be broken down to other meaning. Not to pull out, transubstantiate, boil, unglue, hammer, melt, digest and psychoanalyze, not even to distill but to see and keep what the understanding touches intact—as grapes are round and come in bunches.
>
> To discover and separate these things from the amorphous, the conglomerate normality with which they are surrounded and of which before the act of "creation" each is a part, calls for an eye to draw out that detail which is in itself the thing, to clinch our insight, that is, our understanding, of it.
>
> It is this eye for the thing that most distinguishes Charles Sheeler—and along with it to know that every hair on every body, now or then, in its minute distinctiveness is the same hair, on every body anywhere, at any time, changed as it may be to feather, quill or scale. [Are you following this? It's very funny. I'll read that little thing again because it's really cute.]

The local is the universal. [THE LOCAL IS THE UNIVERSAL.]

Look! that's where painting begins. A bird, up above, flying, may be the essence of it—but a dead canary, with glazed eye, has no less an eye, for that well seen becomes sight and song itself. It is in things that for the artist the power lies, not beyond them. Only where the eye hits does sight occur.

This week someone in class handed me a little poem—perfect illustration of that point:

> The room lies quiet and still.
> His gaze lights on a hair hanging from the lamp
> waving gracefully.

It's a perfect little Williams poem, except in a funny way much lighter, a very late refinement. Everybody get that? Anybody not hear that because they were daydreaming or their minds weren't "clamped down" on objects in present time? Okay, I'll read it one more time.

> The room lies quiet and still.
> His gaze lights on a hair hanging from the lamp
> waving gracefully.

One tiny simple isolated detail—somebody's long hair hanging from a lamp, the guy's in bed? But anyway the room lies quiet and still. Very nicely done.

STUDENT: Where Williams says "similes never are . . . good"—they virtually have no place in "no ideas but in things" except they tend to clutter up an image?

GINSBERG: Yeah.

STUDENT: So, you would say for good poetry—

GINSBERG: Of this mode—

STUDENT: Yeah, of this mode. You would leave them out?

GINSBERG: Yeah, it would be more expressed by the action. That is, I think both Pound and Williams felt that. Of course, they use them occasionally, but try to eliminate the word *like* or *as*—that tactical trick of putting two things together by saying *like* or *as*. If you can do it by just putting thing-facts together without a linking word, if they actually jump together in the mind, then you got it made. You can make a simile if you don't use *like* or *as*. The famous imagist poem by Pound,

> The apparition of these faces in the crowd;
> Petals on a wet, black bough.

"In a Station of the Metro." The point there was that he didn't use "is like"—he said, "The apparition of these faces in the crowd; / Petals on a wet, black bough." So first they revolted against making use of the additional *like* and *as*, the words *like* and *as* which are traditionally used to link anything with anything. So they said if you really want to link things up you got to observe them link themselves up in your mind, you don't "make" a simile.

STUDENT: Are metaphors equally suspect then?

GINSBERG: What's metaphor, I've forgotten.

STUDENT: "Your thighs are apple blossoms."

GINSBERG: Yeah, of course. "Your thighs are appletrees / whose blossoms touch the sky." And the first thing Williams did was have his wife reply, "Which sky?" He opens his poetic career by questioning that use of metaphor. What they substituted was direct "action," direct observation—of course, that was what Hemingway was doing basically.

The key thing for Williams's practice and what he likes in Pound is: "We seek a language which will not be at least a deformation of speech as we know it." Write as you talk, the model for the writing is the rhythm and diction of the speech "as we know it." At least that the poetry not be "a deformation of [that] speech." But "will embody all the advantageous jumps"—advantageous jumps of mind!—jumps of syntax, "swiftnesses, colors, movements of the day . . . THAT WILL AT LEAST NOT EXCLUDE LANGUAGE AS SPOKEN—ALL language (present) as spoken." That was actually for those days quite a big serious discovery, both for Pound and for Williams. Same for us now!

So what I recommend if you want to know how Williams thinks, some of the "Prologue to *Kora in Hell*," probably a little bit on James Joyce, "A Note on the Recent Work of James Joyce" back in 1927, the review of Pound, "Excerpts from a Critical Sketch: *A Draft of XXX Cantos*," "The Work of Gertrude Stein," they're only a few pages each, just little reviews that he wrote for *Contact* magazine, or whoever he was writing for then, *The Nation*. If you want to know about Marianne Moore, his is one of the best essays on Marianne Moore. And the whole "American Background," that long essay on America and Alfred Steiglitz in 1934. And this little "A 1 Pound Stein." Little thing on Sheeler has a little bit more on Americana and imagism. There's a weird review of Carl Sandburg calling his entire range of poetry a featureless desert with interesting poems, but featureless in the sense that in the verse there was no attention paid to the actual composition of verse as speech, so there was no form given to the verse—Williams got more and more interested in some kind of "American measure," or *some* kind of definiteness to the verse forms. Well, there's all these great letters between Pound and Williams. Well, if you want to know how they related, sort of (*Selected Essays*, p.8)—

> . . . God knows I have to work hard enough to escape, not *propagande*, but getting centered in *propagande*. And America? What the h—l do you a blooming foreigner know about the place. Your *père* only penetrated the edge, and you've never been west of Upper Darby, or the Maunchunk switchback.
>
> Would H., with the swirl of the prairie wind in her underwear, or the Virile Sandburg recognize you, an effete easterner as a REAL American? INCONCEIVABLE!!!!!
>
> My dear boy you have never felt the woop of the PEEraries. You have never seen the projecting and protuberant Mts. of the SIerra Nevada. WOT can you know of the country?
>
> You have the naive credulity of a Co. Clare emigrant. But I (*der grosse Ich*) have the virus, the bacillus of the land in my blood, for nearly three bleating centuries.
>
> (Bloody snob. 'eave a brick at 'im!!!) . . .
>
> I was very glad to see your wholly incoherent unamerican poems in the L.R. [*Little Review*]
>
> Of course Sandburg will tell you that you miss the "big drifts," and Bodenheim will object to your not being sufficiently decadent.
>
> You thank your blookin gawd you've got enough Spanish blood to muddy up your mind, and prevent the current American ideation from going through it like a blighted colander.

> The thing that saves your work is opacity, and don't forget it. Opacity is NOT an American quality. Fizz, swish, gabble, and verbiage, these are *echt americanisch.*
>
> And alas, alas, poor old Masters. Look at Oct. *Poetry.*

And so forth. This is Pound to Williams—'cause Pound was born in Hailey, Idaho, and Williams was first generation. When Pound ran off to Europe he was a real American running off, whereas Williams had this sort of guilty first- or second-generation thing of trying—well that's the whole point about Williams, he was a foreigner trying to talk American, he was trying to figure out how people talked, actually. It was his advantage, in a way.

In the early Williams, there's a kind of opaque quality. "To an Old Jaundiced Woman" (*Collected Poems, Vol. I*, pp. 215–6):

O tongue
licking
the sore on
her netherlip

O toppled belly

O passionate cotton
stuck with
matted hair

elsian slobber
upon
the folded handkerchief

I can't die

—moaned the old
jaundiced woman
rolling her
saffron eyeballs

I can't die
I can't die

That's the doctor taking notes, probably on his prescription pad, from the size of the line. Because he did write a lot on his prescription pad. "Elsian!" Elsian is his own personal mythological dumb used slattern

broad who gets fucked up by life. "Some Elsie," some doctor's servant—
"her great / ungainly hips and flopping breasts // addressed to cheap /
jewelry / and rich young men with fine eyes. . . ." "Some Elsie," he says.
So he's made an adjective out it, "elsian slobber."* A poem "To Elsie,"
beginning "The pure products of America / go crazy" (*Collected Poems,
Vol. I*, pp. 217–19). That was his presentation of the karmic situation of
America, actually: "imaginations which have no // peasant traditions to
give them / character" and

> as if the earth under our feet
> were
> an excrement of some sky
>
> and we degraded prisoners
> destined
> to hunger until we eat filth
>
> while the imagination strains
> after deer
> going by fields of goldenrod . . .

STUDENT: Had you read that when you started *Howl?*

GINSBERG: Yes, I had read that—I had that very much in mind when I
wrote *Howl*—I'm glad you saw the correlation, it's his understanding of
the "imagination." That is, his freedom of imagination, his recognition
of the beauteous, hideous necessity of imagination; in imagination at
least we're free. If we're stuck and hemmed in by what *seem* to us
"facts," still there's the heart's imagination and the mind's imagination
of what we actually desire. Here defined as "deer / going by fields of
goldenrod in // the stifling heat of September. . . ." That is out on the open
road. But "as if the earth under our feet / were / an excrement of some
sky // and we degraded prisoners / destined / to hunger until we eat filth,"
seemed to me like the whole karmic condition of America, when I discovered this poem in the fifties.

---

* Editor's Note: The text for this 1975 lecture was the the now out-of-print *Collected Earlier
Poems* (New Directions: 1951). I have adjusted page references throughout the essay to con-
form to the current standard edition, *The Collected Poems* (New Directions, 1986, 1988). In
the current edition, however, this line has been changed from "elsian slobber" to "elysian slobber" in accord with all editions prior to the *Collected Earlier Poems*. In preparing that edition,
Williams cut another line from this poem, so it's unclear whether the change from "elysian" to
"elsian" in the edition used by Ginsberg was a revision or an error.

Another little prophetic turn of sexual imagination, "Horned Purple" (pp. 221–2).

> This is the time of year
> when boys fifteen and seventeen
> wear two horned lilac blossoms
> in their caps—or over one ear
>   [. . .]
> Out of their sweet heads
> dark kisses—rough faces

That's really sweet, the last line, funny thing for him to come to—he finally got the essence of adolescent desirousness, actually the old satyric meaning. Soon after that comes one moment when his attention is totally fixed and concentrated on one object (p. 224).

> so much depends
> upon
>
> a red wheel
> barrow
>
> glazed with rain
> water
>
> beside the white
> chickens

I always figured that "so much depends," means his whole mind depends on the image. Or "so much," a clear apprehension of the entire universe: just being there completely mindful—"I heard a fly buzz—when I died"— that's Emily Dickinson's line.

STUDENT: Your introduction to *Visions of Cody* talked about a karmic hangover in America, what's that mean?

GINSBERG: Somebody lands and deceives the red man and steals his space to begin with. America never did belong to us. So that's why our forefathers were always looking up to English manners and English poetry. Williams finally comes along and has to confront that effect—wrote his long poetic-history book, *In the American Grain*, wherein recognizing how we took over the actual land by force we therefore got this neurosis of not wanting to see the land we had taken, not wanting to actually live here, but wanting to live in a mechanical dream world. With imports from England for thought, meter, poesy, music, philosophy, rather than having to feel the tragic fact that we're trespassers in our own bodies and on our own land. So then Williams was recognizing that fact, urging that we recognize the awkwardness and the weirdness of our presence here, which is why he dug Poe. Thus all his prose poems about other heroes who understood America in his terms.

STUDENT: Similar view to Gary Snyder's *Earth House Hold*?

GINSBERG: Snyder? Well, Williams is one of Snyder's heroes, yeah. I suppose Snyder actually belongs to that lineage, they met actually, turned each other on, and Williams noticed Snyder's poetry later.

In "Rapid Transit" Williams sounds like Philip Whalen (pp. 231–2). (Actually compare this with a poem in the Don Allen anthology by Whalen, "Big High Song for Somebody.") "Rapid Transit":

Somebody dies every four minutes
in New York State—

To hell with you and your poetry—
You will rot and be blown
through the next solar system
with the rest of the gases—

What the hell do you know about it?

AXIOMS

Don't get killed

Careful Crossing Campaign
Cross Crossings Cautiously
　　　　[. . .]
Interborough Rapid Transit Co.

That particular poem probably influenced Whalen—randomness and the humor, composing out of the subway map and subway signs.

"The Descent of Winter" (p. 291) is a classic exercise again in "sketching" like the one we had in "Sunday" (p. 396). Trungpa suggested taking a walk in Boulder and watching rather than analyzing details, and then I read, following that, Williams's series of simple sketches. Here he's a little older, with a series of clever vignettes—little fragments, he's not even trying to finish a poem anymore, just trying to get a little detail. There's no hope in writing unless you can accumulate many, many tiny details, tiny shells of coral accumulate, an island slowly forming, to wait for others to drop their shit on it and make it habitable. You know, he's saying you have to build up an entire poetic universe of detail. "And there's a little blackboy / in a doorway / scratching his wrists / . . . " So that's as far as he'd gotten by the last lines "October tenth / 1927" (p. 293).

> In the dead weeds a rubbish heap
> aflame . . .
>   [. . .]
> What chance have the old?.
>   [. . .]
> Their feet hurt, they are weak
> they should not have to suffer
> as younger people must and do
> there should be a truce for them

The object there is his own compassionate thoughts about old folks. Jumping to page 302:

> 11/1
>
> The moon, the dried weeds
> and the Pleiades—
>
> Seven feet tall
> the dark, dried weedstalks
> make a part of the night
> a red lace
> on the blue milky sky
>
> Write —
> by a small lamp
>
> the Pleiades are almost
> nameless
> and the moon is tilted
> and halfgone
>
> And in runningpants and
> with ecstatic, aesthetic faces
> on the illumined
> signboard are leaping
> over printed hurdles and

"$1/4$ of their energy comes from bread"

two
gigantic highschool boys
ten feet tall

A bread advertisement, it's a very funny combo: a billboard advertisement off a highway in New Jersey surrounded by dried weeds.

STUDENT: Did he get turned on by photography, by stills?

GINSBERG: Yeah, that's why he was hanging around with Alfred Steiglitz. He probably, I think, took that as a form, sketching or still photography. What I like are the almost minimal little sketch details because they're sort of the vipasyana practice that anybody can do. And occasionally then there'll be some burst of a larger ambition, like on page 308:

11/8

O river of my heart polluted
and defamed I have compared you
to that other lying in
the red November grass
beginning to be cleaned now
from factory pollution

Though at night a watchman
must still prowl lest some paid hand
open the waste sluices—

That river will be clean
before ever you will be

STUDENT: Couldn't you say then why not take a photograph of it?

GINSBERG: Well, because you're beginning, you're practicing with language, to see if you can build a coral island out of all the little details. To see if you can train yourself in speech consciousness. You're practicing a speech consciousness, not an eyeball consciousness. Photography would be an eyeball consciousness. The poem would be speech consciousness, a refinement of speech.

STUDENT: [*inaudible*] . . . "Camera . . . framing?"

GINSBERG: Framing, definitely, framing your *mind* in this case, framing the language of your mind. You remember way at the very beginning he dipped his hand in the "filthy Passaic" and the Passaic River in Paterson consented to him being the muse of the river and years later, 1927, "O river of my heart polluted . . . that river will be. . . ." Talking about the river of my heart.

But then there's a funny outburst, more like 1960s. He gets political, the Sacco/Vanzetti case. A thing called "Impromptu: the Suckers" (p. 270), which is a really prophetic sort of anti-police-state radical rant for Williams, very "vulgar" for Williams. Full of energy and full of good intentions, and information actually; what's interesting is the straightforward citizenly stubborn toughness here. The "sucker" is the entire nation at this point, the guys who voted for Nixon or the guys who voted for or were in favor of executing two anarchist fellows accused of a bomb plot, Nicola Sacco and Bartolomeo Vanzetti.

Impromptu: The Suckers

Take it out in vile whisky, take it out
in lifting your skirts to show your silken
crotches; it is this that is intended.
You are it. Your pleas will always be denied.
You too will always go up with the two guys,
scapegoats to save the Republic and
especially the State of Massachusetts. The
Governor says so and you ain't supposed
to ask for details—

Your case has been reviewed by high-minded
and unprejudiced observers (like hell
they were!) the president of a great
university, the president of a noteworthy
technical school and a judge too old to sit
on the bench, men already rewarded for
their services to pedagogy and the enforcement
of arbitrary statutes. In other words
pimps to tradition—

Why in hell didn't they choose some other
kind of "unprejudiced adviser" for their
death council? instead of sticking to that
autocratic strain of Boston backwash, except
that the council was far from unprejudiced

but the product of a rejected, discredited
class long since outgrown except for use in
courts and school, and that they
wanted it so—

Why didn't they choose at least one decent
Jew or some fair-minded Negro or anybody
but such a triumvirate of inversion, the
New England aristocracy, bent on working off
a grudge against you, Americans, you
are the suckers, you are the ones who will
be going up on the eleventh to get the current
shot into you, for the glory of the state
and the perpetuation of abstract justice—

And all this in the face of the facts: that
the man who swore, and deceived the jury
willfully by so doing, that the bullets found
in the bodies of the deceased could be
identified as having been fired from the pistol
of one of the accused—later
acknowledged that he could not so identify
them; that the jurors now seven years after
the crime do not remember the details and
have wanted to forget them; that the
prosecution has never succeeded in
apprehending the accomplices nor in connecting
the prisoners with any of the loot stolen—

The case is perfect against you, all the
documents say so—in spite of the fact that
it is reasonably certain that you were not
at the scene of the crime, shown, quite as
convincingly as the accusing facts in the
court evidence, by better reasoning to have
been committed by someone else with whom
the loot can be connected and among whom the
accomplices can be found—

It's no use, you are Americans, just the dregs.
It's all you deserve. You've got the cash,
what the hell do you care? You've got
nothing to lose. You are inheritors of a great
tradition. My country right or wrong!
You do what you're told to do. You don't
answer back the way Tommy Jeff did or Ben

> Frank or Georgie Washing. I'll say you
> don't. You're civilized. You let your
> betters tell you where you get off. Go
> ahead—
>
> But after all, the thing that swung heaviest
> against you was that you were scared when
> they copped you. Explain that you
> nature's nobleman! For you know that every
> American is innocent and at peace in his
> own heart. He hasn't a damned thing to be
> afraid of. He knows the government is for
> him. Why, when a cop steps up and grabs
> you at night you just laugh and think it's
> a hell of a good joke—
>
> This is what was intended from the first.
> So take it out in your rotten whiskey and
> silk underwear. That's what you get out of
> it. But put it down in your memory that this
> is the kind of stuff that they can't get away
> with. It is there and it's loaded. No one
> can understand what makes the present age
> what it is. They are mystified by certain
> insistences.

Well, that's like a great tirade, a model for dealing right now with the Wounded Knee trial or any of the recent "dissident" conspiracy trials, present police-state situations. And Williams's take on it, with all the details of the Sacco/Vanzetti case and then his peroration including case-facts, his energy on it is one of the few great political common sense breakthroughs, I mean it's also *vulnerable* Williams getting mad and angry like a good citizen. A funny model poem with weird prophetic seriousness—"Why when a cop steps up and grabs / you at night you just laugh and think it's / a hell of a good joke—" I always thought this was a really amazing poem for him, following "The pure products of America / go crazy," those two. Apparently at this time he got prophetic about America.

STUDENT: What do you think about the form of that? 'Cause it's very interesting in that sense, broken down as a set of paragraphs.

GINSBERG: I bet you it was written in prose and he chopped it up, it'd be interesting to know. It looks like, oh, blank verse, just the eye on the page makes it look like blank verse. Of course, the actual speech is much more variable than Shakespeare's blank verse. I don't know how he arrived at this, it's one of the very first pieces of that kind, with a thick line. Except "A Morning Imagination of Russia" and the other thing I read from *Paterson* originally, is where he gets philosophical. "No ideas but in things" has the same form—a thick line on the page, 'cause he's got a lot to say, a lot of talking to do.

That was the one thing that turned me on to my own style—I think it's one of the grosser elements in Williams, but it's also one of the most charming things he did—that he let himself open and he laid out that sort of vulnerable angry tirade. It also shows you a tradition, there was a breakthrough in consciousness in America all the way back then in the late twenties and the early thirties, of this kind of police-state paranoia, heavy metal Burroughsian awareness. It was pretty strong then among anarchists, among the literary bohemians of that day. That radical awareness of the difference between a political front as presented by judges and university trustees, and what was actually going on in the back room of courts and jails. It's amazing how solid his perception is there and how valid it is now.

That long poem of Williams's was a political statement, a sudden angry testament prophetic of later police-state tendencies in America. The Sacco/Vanzetti case: two Italian fish peddlers from Boston were set up, on a fake bombing charge, and executed. It was the first blood in this era of state murder at the beginning of the Great Cold War. It was a big thing, all the intellectuals got involved, including Williams, it was one of the big causes of the radical left.

STUDENT: Woody Guthrie did an album of a lot of songs about it.

GINSBERG: Yeah. There were songs, books, poems, my father wrote a poem that was in *The New Masses*. Edna St. Vincent Millay wrote a poem called "Justice Denied in Massachusetts" once they were killed.

That political strain comes into Williams—there's a description of the Capitol building in Washington, his aesthetic comment on the vision of America conjured by a collage of elements—paintings, sculpture, architectural construction—at Washington Capitol (pp. 255–58): "It Is a Living Coral // a trouble // archaically fettered / to produce . . . dead //

among the wreckage / sickly green." That was his "character" of the Capitol; a national portrait done in the official detail using the architecture of the Capitol building: as near as you could get, if you were an imagist using "no ideas but in things" and wanting to do a commentary on the state of the nation.

More into his real genre, "Hemmed-in Males" (p. 273); it's one that I always thought was like the best of poor old Paterson or Rutherford. "The saloon is gone up the creek / . . . there's no place // any more for me to go now / except home—" Real sympathetic and sweet. "You can laugh at him without his / organs but that's the way with / a river when it wants to // drown you. . . ."

A little exercise called "This Florida, 1924," (p. 359) gets back to his preoccupation with finding little rhythmical turns in his own speech usable as poetry. The theme is his imagination wandering off while he's in the real Florida doing a real job; actually, dreaming of Florida while doing his job there as a doctor. But listening to the sounds. The very last lines are classic American speech, lines he thought rhythmically most interesting. It has the rhythm *da-da-da da-da-da-da-da-da / da-da.* You'll recognize it when you get to it. "This Florida, 1924 . . . / Peggy has a little albumen / in hers—" Actually, so he's got this long disquisition on "orange"—"Rather, Hibiscus, / let me examine." Because he's doing his pees, examining all the little pee samples to see who's got what, kidney trouble. "Peggy has a little albumen / in hers—" That's the last phrase of the poem.

Now the great poem on the tree. Remember I paraphrased the *Kora in Hell* Prologue in order to describe one tree of all the trees on earth, to separate out that one tree that you want to describe (if you're trying to write a song lyric and you want to put in something real sharp, a visual image, that people will remember, or poem) you have to rely on the specific detail that differs it from all objects of its kind. And his most interesting tree I think is "Young Sycamore." You completely see a tree with a number of little details, I think it's the acme of tree description. Randall Jarrell noticed that Williams was really conversant with trees, remember, "The trees / are become / beasts fresh-risen / from the sea—" Jarrell said Williams has turned more people into trees (or more trees into people, whichever)—than any other poet. Odd, that Williams, supposed to be this "difficult modernist," was actually so well connected with old-fashioned pastoral nature. "Young Sycamore" (p. 266) begins really nice. "I must tell you." "I must tell you." The doctor in his office, "I must tell you." Who is he talking to? You, actually. "I must tell *you /* this young tree. . . ." And it's all one fast notation, probably three breaths I would say. There are only two, well maybe one two three four five breaths, I would guess. I'll try reading it again with five breaths according to his scoring.

Young Sycamore

I must tell you
this young tree
whose round and firm trunk
between the wet

pavement and the gutter
(where water
is trickling) rises
bodily

into the air with
one undulant
thrust half its height—
and then

dividing and waning
sending out
young branches on
all sides—

hung with cocoons—
it thins
till nothing is left of it
but two

eccentric knotted
twigs
bending forward
hornlike at the top

That's the right way. He's given the scoring, there's a little parenthesis which requires another breath after "half its height—," there's another dash after "young branches on / all sides—" and from "hung with cocoons" to end "hornlike at the top" it's all one breath. So there's a lot going on in these stanzas which are relatively even four-line stanzas, the poem is arranged into four-line parts.

Here's a funny little photograph at home called "Poem"—obviously it's something he noticed and wrote down, realized later was a poem, so he called it a "Poem" (p. 352):

> As the cat
> climbed over
> the top of
>
> the jamcloset
> first the right
> forefoot
>
> carefully
> then the hind
> stepped down
>
> into the pit of
> the empty
> flowerpot

It's mostly a line of three syllables each. In one stanza the first line is "the jamcloset" which is four, but then the third and last line of that stanza is only two syllables, so he balanced it out. Are you following me? It's basically a line of three syllables. And if you're writing any kind of short-line poetry like that, counting syllables is one good way to base your line. It gives you a funny little regularity, funny measure, almost unconscious, you wouldn't notice it unless you were interested in trying to find out what's going on. But it does give a kind of backbone. Not yet the variable foot, you see. Does everybody follow what I'm saying about counting syllables? (Marianne Moore was the great lady of syllable count.)

My father's favorite Williams poem (page 241):

The Jungle

> It is not the still weight
> of the trees, the
> breathless interior of the wood,
> tangled with wrist-thick
>
> vines, the flies, reptiles,
> the forever fearful monkeys
> screaming and running
> in the branches—

>   but
> a girl waiting
> shy, brown, soft-eyed—
> to guide you
>   Upstairs, sir.

And then, like a Chinese poem (except a Chinese poet compares the fallen lotus blossom floating down the river to the fading away of charm of cheek of his lady), Williams going from ward to ward of the Paterson General Hospital had other flowers or blossoms to observe, here in "Between Walls" (p. 453):

> the back wings
> of the
>
> hospital where
> nothing
>
> will grow lie
> cinders
>
> in which shine
> the broken
>
> pieces of a green
> bottle

With Chinese poetry in mind, that tradition of observation, he's looked into that back-ass place of every building that everybody knows from working as a secretary in trucking companies to going to high school too late. So he's comparing that green bottle to the living flower—of his imagination or of his perception. Phil, you have something relevant?

STUDENT: Well, I was thinking of the other poem. I wondered if every word was absolutely necessary and weighted and considered, right? He goes off on this discursive thing. . . .

GINSBERG: Yes, because it's not a real jungle he's talking about, this guy is talking about an imaginary jungle. So he's got "forever fearful monkeys screaming" and so on. That's obviously an exaggeration. When he gets to what he actually sees, "but / a girl waiting . . . sir" that's where he gets more precise. The actual description of the jungle is like a bullshit jungle.

But he's also saying the *real* jungle of emotions where you're trapped by wild beasties is the actual everyday situation, not the imaginary jungle in the Amazon that you read about in W. H. Hudson or can imagine from the movies. So he's got a movie jungle there with naturally imprecise sloppy language a little bit, he's never been in the jungle.

STUDENT: Well, I liked it myself. I'm just saying that that kind of throws another light on what Pound was. . . .

GINSBERG: Yeah, but I'm just pointing out that he's talking about an imaginary jungle, that it's not an observed jungle, and that everybody's scared of imaginary jungles but the *real* jungle they see in front of them is the considerable one. Obviously, that's not like a practice trip, that description of the jungle with wrist-thick vines is very vague, "flies and reptiles," pretty much a Rutherford jungle, isn't a jungle of somebody who's really been around a jungle.

In "Nantucket" (p. 372) there's a little portrait, not of a person but a room with all the perfect nostalgia of a specific room.

> Flowers through the window
> lavender and yellow
>
> changed by white curtains—
> Smell of cleanliness—
>
> Sunshine of late afternoon—
> On the glass tray
>
> a glass pitcher, the tumbler
> turned down, by which
>
> a key is lying—And the
> immaculate white bed

That's real New England island-perfect boarding house. And well, yeah, the poem I like best to illustrate his method is something he left literally as a note for his wife, which after he reread in the morning he put in the book as another poem (p. 372).

This Is Just to Say

> I have eaten
> the plums

that were in
the icebox

and which
you were probably
saving
for breakfast

Forgive me
they were delicious
so sweet
and so cold

I think that's one of his greatest exemplary poems, because finally it's where life and poetry are identical, there's no separation, that the note that he would write to communicate to his wife is identical to what he would put in a book to communicate to the eternal.

STUDENT: [*inaudible*] . . . See everything as poetry?

GINSBERG: Well, everything *is* poetry, to begin with, if you see it. He begins to see everything finally. And naturally it becomes poetry. Which is the point, again—making a parallel to the lectures going on upstairs, on the iconography of Buddhism, where the upstairs guru is pointing out that if you *look*, and if you're attentive without resentment, every noise becomes punctuation in the big mantra and every little movement has a meaning of its own. (You know that old song, [*singing*] "Every little movement has a meaning of its own" about the belly dancers of the vampish twenties, you know.)

Yeah, so there's a point, as Rinpoche was pointing out, where one's perception of everyday life becomes clear because there's no obstacle of trying to impose a thought on it, or there's no obstacle trying to impose a poem on it. No obstacle trying to impose another world on it. So that it becomes a complete absolute world in which "the natural object is always an adequate symbol" of itself and in which every object shines out with its own significance, a meaning to which every movement has relationship—the example Trungpa had given was the ground insects in the parking lot, some twirling around, some zigzagging, some going in a straight line, some eventually stopping and going off on a tangent. They all follow their own self-ultimate fatal paths and an observant person seeing them would be struck by the humor and curiosity of so much individuality finding its own way. Or a person wanting to impose an idea would say, "That's nothing but a bunch of insects, why bother to look at them, why bother perceiving them?" And about some cold plums in the icebox, what's so poetic about that? But the clarity and preciseness of the perception as well as the humor and generosity of his relationship with his wife, revealed by the tone and exactness of the note that he sends her, makes it a picture of their entire domestic life and psychological relationship. That she got these plums which she says, "Save for breakfast, don't take in the middle of the night." And him knowing and saying, "which you were probably saving for breakfast, forgive me." He's stolen the plums from his wife, "Forgive me / they were delicious." So you have their sexual relationship set up actually by that little thing. I mean you have their personal, emotive, role-playing set-up and then you have the doctor who's coming down in the middle of the night (as in the early poem noticing "a glass filled with parsley—crisped green . . . on the grooved drain-board" and standing there in his pajamas and turning on the spigot and waiting for the water to freshen before it gets nice and cold for his drink. Noticing how the water "freshens.") So there's a doctor in the kitchen again, but totally awake with beating mind, "Forgive me / they were delicious / so sweet / and so cold." Or, actually he was probably just tired and wrote it down, but in the morning he realized how precise the writing was.

I want to finish now with a little Williams, summing it all up—"Birds and Flowers"—so suggesting a still life (pp. 326–28).

> Nothing is lost! The white
> shellwhite
> glassy, linenwhite, crystalwhite
> crocuses with orange centers
> the purple crocus with
> an orange center, the yellow
> crocus with a yellow center—
>   [. . .]
>   Though the eye
> turns inward, the mind
> has spread its embrace—in
> a wind that
> roughs the stiff petals—
> More! the particular flower is
> blossoming . . .

So—that's what he was trying to do, get that particular flower of perception blossoming in America, trying to find an American language, using American local diction, trying to find the rhythms of his own talk, "Peggy has a little albumen in hers," ah, trying to compose poems that are indistinguishable from our ordinary speech, and working with perceptions that are indistinguishable from the actual perceptions of our ordinary mind; but which when recognized, and appreciated consciously, transform the entire feeling of existence to a totally new sympathetic universe where we're at home, where we're playful, where we're generous, because the mind overflows with its perceptions, and the perceptions are all generous because they're not blocked by anger. Actually the beginning of this poetic alchemy, as Williams says, is: "A new world is only a new mind." And a new mind is only new words. Or a new mind in poetics is only a new set of words equivalent to those you're actually able to use with your mouth when you're talking—so you don't twist your mouth, and twist your brain, and twist your so-called soul, to strain for an effect of a universe that isn't there, but are talking plainly about what you see in front of you that is there. In that way you don't create paranoia, you dispel paranoia, because you are reaffirming, through clearly presenting your perceptions, the very same perceptions in the minds and eyes of others. So that finally it does come down to what Plato originally said—"When the mode of music changes, the walls of the city shake." When the mode, here of prosody, returns to its normal order, there then begins a new direct perception in the soul, so that "noble is changed to no bull," so that you can see through hallucinated language, you have something to compare hallucinated language with, and you can tell what language rises out of direct contact with phenomena as distinct from language that rises from overheated imagination or desire-to-impress by writing something sounding "poetical." Williams becomes a standard for morality, in a sense, or for a normal state of mind, a standard you can measure your own perceptions and sanity against, measure your own poetry against, measure your own glimpses of what you see, what you recognize of what you see. Thus actually Willlams is the true hero of the first half of the American century, carrying on the work of Whitman.

Bill Zavatsky

The Voice of the Poet
William Carlos Williams on and off the Page

My first reading of William Carlos Williams left me stunned by the sheer volume of physical reality that he could pack into a poem. In my own poetry I had learned to go inside myself, all right, to seize the crazy images that bubbled up from my unconscious. But the things that I lived with every day seemed to elude my grasp. Where were the portraits of my family, the snapshots of my friends, the little yard in front of my house that I grew up playing in, the flowers that my grandmother tended, the pleasures and shocks that I experienced in and out of the classroom?

In the Catholic schools I had attended, nearly all of the poems that we studied were in fixed forms, rhymed and metered. There wasn't room for a troublemaker like William Carlos Williams, who had abandoned those constraints. When I began to try to write poetry, during my sophomore year in high school, there weren't many directions in which to turn.

The world toward which my eyes had been directed for the first twelve years of my education was not this one, but the Other World of the angels and the saints. It was the world of the Idea, which Williams had succinctly rejected in his famous dictum, "No ideas but in things." (A corollary notion which I also had to battle suggested that poetry was not so much a question of hard work as of divine inspiration.) If only I could have heard the NBC radio show called "Anthology" in 1954, when Williams told his interviewer:

> It occurs to me that I might give some more advice to young poets. . . . It is not to talk in a heightened manner, but to use the common language of the street, or of your home, which your mother and father speak. If they [young poets] would only try to get some sort of arrangement in the words that they hear, and speak of just the things that concern them every day, and try to realize them intensely and vividly, they'll probably make a poem—if they have any poetry in their soul.[1]

That was advice I could have made use of! But it wasn't until college that Williams opened the door to the world for me. Kenneth Koch, in his modern poetry course at Columbia, required his students to imitate the poets that we studied as well as to write short papers about their poems. I remember being up all night working on my Williams poem, ecstatic, realizing that I could use *everything* that was coming at me as I wrote: the feel of the sheet-metal kitchen table where I sat, the blue dawn beginning to leak through the airshaft, the scratching noise of my pencil—everything! If you can look at the world this way, the way that Williams looked at it, everything that exists—"ugly" or "beautiful"—is an offering that we can love, or hate, but certainly write about.

Just as Williams's poems brought me closer to the world, the materials that I discuss below bring us closer to William Carlos Williams the man. These recordings and images encompass Williams's entire life, from his unhappy childhood to his first poem, written out of a shattering experience that came after a high school track practice during which he strained his heart and found himself, on doctor's orders, forever forbidden to do anything more strenuous than to take long walks. He happily recited those first lines whenever he had the opportunity, and on five different recorded occasions:

A black, black cloud
flew over the sun
driven by fierce flying
rain.[2]

The poem had supplied him with a tremendous release from his sorrow, Williams said. In it we can see the clarity, imagery, and passion that would mark his mature style, but from the books and tapes listed below we also learn of the long detour that Williams would have to take through the English classics of the Palgrave anthology, Keats, and Whitman before he could reclaim himself. We hear of the English father and Puerto Rican mother, the years of medical study, the friendships with Ezra Pound, Marianne Moore, other poets, and painters, the work on the little magazines of the period, the continual struggle to get published, the shaky, extraordinary marriage to Florence ("Flossie") Herman, the grueling medical practice in Rutherford and Passaic, New Jersey, that was nevertheless essential to him as a writer, the post-war years of triumph, when his long poem *Paterson* brought him international acclaim, and the heart attack and strokes that lashed him for the last fifteen years of his life but never destroyed his will.

Autobiography and Print Interviews

The Autobiography of William Carlos Williams (New York: New Directions, 1967). 402 pp.

Interviews with William Carlos Williams: "Speaking Straight Ahead." Edited with an introduction by Linda Welshimer Wagner (New York: New Directions, 1976). 108 pp.

I Wanted to Write a Poem: The Autobiography of the Works of a Poet. Reported and edited by Edith Heal (New York: New Directions, revised edition, 1978). 100 pp.

We have long been rich in information that has come directly from Williams himself. Though his friend H. D. produced several memoirs, he was the only one of the "classical moderns" to write an autobiography. Though it contains errors of memory, Williams's self-examination is still highly readable. The opening chapters, with their pinpoint remembrances of childhood, are extraordinary, and will stimulate students and teachers to remember their own early years.

Williams may also be the American modernist who granted the most interviews. Late in his life he collaborated on a delightful and informative career retrospective (*I Wanted to Write a Poem*, with Edith Heal), and Linda Wagner's *Interviews with William Carlos Williams: "Speaking Straight Ahead"* draws on a number of the taped conversations that we can now hear, most in their totality, in *The Collected Recordings* (see Audiotapes, below). Viewers may be familiar with snippets of them that were used on the sound track of the *Voices and Visions* Public Television documentary called *William Carlos Williams*.

Videotapes

Voices and Visions: William Carlos Williams. (1988). 60 minutes. Directed by Richard P. Rogers; written and produced by Jill Janows. Mystic Fire Audio. Mail order: P.O. Box 422, New York, NY 10012-0008. Telephone order (and catalogue): 800-292-9001.

William Carlos Williams: A Machine Made of Words. (1996). 30 minutes. Directed and photographed by Colin Still; edited by Anna Price. Optic Nerve, 5 Vanbrugh Hill, London SE3 7UE. Write or call for price: 0181-856-2642; Fax: 0181-319-8901.

William Carlos Williams is perhaps the best of the dozen-or-so television documentaries produced in the 1980s for the *Voices and Visions* series about American poets, which includes programs on Whitman, Pound, Eliot, Stevens, Bishop, Langston Hughes, Hart Crane, and others. Here we are in the capable hands of critics Marjorie Perloff and Hugh Kenner, joined by Robert Coles (who accompanied Dr. Williams on house calls when Coles was a medical student) and Williams's longtime publisher James Laughlin. Featured, too, is the ineffable Allen Ginsberg, who reads and comments on a number of the poems (giving a stunning interpretation of "To Elsie"), and who takes us to view the Passaic Falls in Paterson. The poet's son William Eric Williams, also a physician who lived and practiced medicine in the family home, speaks affectionately of his father and the family, and walks us through the house. Animated sequences ("The Great Figure" and "This Is Just to Say") enliven the documentary. The poems (mostly read by Williams) are also effectively "dramatized" as the camera makes use of the New Jersey landscape on which the poet focused. This film will immeasurably help high school and college students to understand what Williams was all about. (Explicit documentary footage of a childbirth may place it out of bounds for younger viewers.)

Colin Still's half-hour documentary was made for Channel 4 Television in Great Britain as part of its *Modern American Poets* series. *William Carlos Williams: A Machine Made of Words* is a superior piece of filmmaking. Unlike the *Voices and Visions* documentary, which also stresses the life, Still's film relies more on dramatizations of the poems and other poets' assessments of Williams, including commentary from Ginsberg, Michael McClure, Jane Hirshfield, and Kenneth Koch. (Ginsberg's masterful gloss of "No ideas but in things": "What it means, basically, is that it is important to present your ideas through the medium of things observed that represent the ideas.") Still is a master cinematographer, and his colors and images are gorgeous. While the film has been created in the image of the *Voices and Visions* Williams program, it contains marvelous moments, especially in the editing. "By the Road to the

Contagious Hospital," for example, cuts between several poets (who read and comment on the poem) with Williams's own reading voice, as a model-T Ford (the poet's first automobile) trundles around the Jersey marshlands. And there is a touching glimpse of a very old Williams in home movie footage, tethered to Flossie.

Audiotapes

William Carlos Williams Reads. Recorded 1954, issued 1957. 43 minutes. HarperAudio, 10 E. 53 St., New York, NY 10022. (212) 207-7000; Fax: (212) 207-7759; email: harperaudio@harpercollins.com. Note: This is the recording originally made in 1954 by Williams for the Caedmon record label. It is also available in *The Collected Recordings* (tape 11, below).

The Spoken Arts Treasury of 100 Modern American Poets, Volume II. Spoken Arts (1978). The fifteen Williams poems read by the poet on this cassette are selected from the recordings made for the Library of Congress in 1945. For the complete recordings see *The Collected Recordings* (tape 1, below). Other poets on this tape include Wallace Stevens, Witter Bynner, Max Eastman, and Louis Untermeyer.

Voices and Visions: William Carlos Williams. (1988). 60 minutes. Mystic Fire Audio. Mail order: P.O. Box 422, New York, NY 10012-0008. Telephone order (and catalogue): (800) 292-9001. Slightly edited sound track of the *Voices and Visions* video documentary.

William Carlos Williams: The People and the Stones: Selected Poems. (1991). 62 minutes. Watershed Tapes. A first-rate anthology derived from *The Collected Recordings* (see below). Among the selections are "Tract," "Danse Russe," "The Red Wheelbarrow," and excerpts from *Paterson.* Order from Poets' Audio Center: Fax: (202) 722-9106; phone: (800) 366-9105. Internet/email: give them your daytime phone number; mail: 6925 Willow Street NW, Suite 201, Washington, DC 20012-2023. The Watershed catalogue is accessible on the Internet's World Wide Web at http://www.writer.org/pac/pac03.htm.

William Carlos Williams: The Collected Recordings. 20 Volumes. General Editor: Richard Swigg; Editor: Richard J. Baker (1992–1993). Keele University.

- 1. Library of Congress, 1945, 1947.
- 2. National Council of Teachers of English/Columbia Records/ Richard Wirtz Emerson/University of California, Los Angeles: 1942, 1949, 1950.
- 3. Interview with John W. Gerber, 1950.
- 4. Eyvind Earle/University of Buffalo/Kenneth Burke/National Institute of Arts and Letters: 1950, 1951.
- 5. Interviews with Mary Margaret McBride, 1950, 1951, 1954.
- 6. Harvard University, 1951.
- 7. Princeton University, 1952.
- 8. Hanover College, 1952.
- 9. 92nd Street YM-YWHA Poetry Center, 1954.
- 10. NBC/ Voice of America, 1954.
- 11. Caedmon, 1954.
- 12. Washington University, St. Louis, 1955.
- 13. University of California, Berkeley, 1955.
- 14. University of California, Santa Barbara, 1955.
- 15. University of California, Los Angeles, 1955.
- 16. Eyvind Earle, 1955.
- 17. Yale University, 1955.
- 18. University of Puerto Rico (excerpt)/Interview with John Wingate: 1956, 1957.
- 19. Interviews with Walter Sutton, 1960.
- 20. Interviews with Walter Sutton (concluded); Interviews with Stanley Koehler: 1960, 1962.

A booklet entitled *William Carlos Williams: The Collected Recordings—An Introduction,* by Richard Swigg, with essay, indices, and a transcript of the Koehler interview is provided on purchase of five or more recordings. Tapes are available individually or as a complete set, with the following exceptions: cassette 9 may be bought only with one other or more recordings; cassettes 19 and 20 may be bought only as a pair.

Inquiries to Department of English, Keele University, Keele, Staffordshire ST5 5BG, UK. From the U.S., telephone 011-44-1-782-621111; fax 011-44-1-782-713468.

A catalogue of this and other cassette publications is available. A full listing of the poems read by Williams and topic headings of the discussions on each cassette may be found in the catalogue or on the Internet at the Keele University site: http://www.keele.ac.uk/depts/en/archII.htm.

"Hear the voice of the Bard!" cried Blake, though his cry rang out from the page. In this century we have been able to hear the voices of our modern and contemporary poets, and in the front rank of those coming across loudest and clearest stands William Carlos Williams. With the invention of the long-playing record and the audiocassette, poetry's democratization proceeds at an accelerating pace.

The voice of Williams is an American voice. "We talk American, we don't talk English," he told his audience at UCLA in 1950. Compared to his energetic, "regular guy" delivery, even Frost seems mannered, cranky. The slower-than-slow Wallace Stevens sounds positively ethereal. In Ezra Pound's bardic quaver we can hear the echo of Yeats; Eliot imitates the intonation of the Englishman. But Williams kept his ear at street-level, aiming bits of palaver like "Atta boy! Atta boy!" at the mailman who ought to be bringing him money ("To Greet a Letter-Carrier"). At other moments he sculpted what he heard into edifices of sound that achieve an indigenous nobility, like the lament (eventually called "To Elsie") that begins, "The pure products of America / go crazy—." It is fitting that Williams has become the poet most available on recordings; the American language was everything to him, as important as his full-time medical practice.

Williams comes across strong and sweet and feisty and funny on these recordings until strokes begin to batter him in 1951, increasingly disabling him. Nevertheless, I love even the recordings made at the poet's home in June of 1954. Here is the old doctor, occasionally missing a word or stumbling on a syllable, often sounding exhausted. And yet his voice can lift into passion, more affecting in many ways than in any of his other recordings because we know the cost of it. (After the worst strokes, Williams had to relearn how to speak and write.) Featured are his standbys ("The Botticellian Trees," "The Yachts," "The Catholic Bells," "Smell!" "Primrose," "Between Walls") as well as the astounding poems that he was writing during the late '40s and '50s, including some of his last great works ("The Descent," "To Daphne and Virginia," "For Eleanor and Bill Monahan," "The Host," and an excerpt from "Asphodel, That Greeny Flower," then known as "Work in Progress"). One could survive the personal holocaust and still have a voice to speak with. That broken voice, however diminished, is of value too. With it Williams teaches us what it means to grow old, to suffer, and to triumph as he approaches the end, "The Descent," he called it, that is "made up of despairs / and without accomplishment" but that "realizes a new awakening: / which is a reversal / of despair."

Watershed Tapes offers a superb miscellany of Williams called *William Carlos Williams: The People and the Stones: Selected Poems.* (Here are the great poems "Tract," "Danse Russe," "The Red Wheelbarrow," "Perpetuum Mobile: The City," as well as "Choral: The Pink Church" and an excerpt from the magnificent "Asphodel." Two snippets include Williams in conversation with Mary Margaret McBride on her radio program (1954), where he recites his first poem. There are also 1945 recordings from the Library of Congress archives and a number of gems drawn from hitherto unavailable private collections. The second side features selections from *Paterson*, Williams's epic poem. This tape selects from the massive anthology published by Keele University, serving as a kind of sampler of it.

Which will serve to introduce *William Carlos Williams: The Collected Recordings*, an extraordinary anthology of Williams readings, lectures, formal and informal interviews, and tapes made in friends' homes between 1942 and 1962, assembled by Richard Swigg. Professor Swigg ought to be awarded one of those medals that the President now and then bestows on those who have done great service to the cultural life of our country. These twenty volumes make Williams the most available American poet (and perhaps world poet) on recording.

There are many wonderful moments in *The Collected Recordings*. Asked by radio talk show host Mary Margaret McBride to explain the famous "Red Wheelbarrow" poem that he has just recited, Williams offers a wonderful gloss. "I wrote that. And then, of course, I sat down to think about it," the poet says. "And what did you think?" asks McBride. "What did I think?" replies Williams, laughing. "I wondered what it meant. Until a lady from Boston wrote and said, 'Dr. Williams, that is a charming poem. But what in the world does it mean?' And then I began to realize that it meant exactly the same as the first two lines of *Endymion*: 'A thing of beauty is a joy forever.'" (Of course the good doctor has cut his beloved Keats's line in two, but the point is there.) This is the best interpretation of that famous little poem that I've ever heard. Indeed, with the exception of the Koehler interviews, done not long before he died and during which the poet shows the serious effects of his cerebral accidents, Williams is an ebullient, good-humored, eloquent, and sometimes irascible interviewee. He talks to McBride with great candor about his childhood ("I was very unhappy"), and the Gerber interview (transcribed in Wagner) is a delight as well as a trove of biographical information. (I played it for my high school seniors, who loved it.) Here Williams tells his interlocutor: "The theory is that you can make a poem out of *anything*. You don't have to have conventionally poetic material. Anything that is *felt*, and that is felt deeply, or deeply enough, or even that gives amusement, is material for art." In the interview, Williams tells the story behind "This Is Just to Say," the famous poem about the plums.

Many of the readings also feature Williams's commentaries and off-the-cuff remarks that now seem invaluable. At Harvard in 1951, Williams tells his audience, "If it ain't a pleasure, it ain't a poem!" Though he generally eschewed explanations of his poems, he also points out, with great charm, "You should never explain a poem, but it always helps, nevertheless. You want to *get* it!" We feel that Williams is always tickled to be reading his poems, even so late in life, after the long years during which only a handful of poets and writers knew or cared about his work. And upon delivering two short poems to the Harvard crowd, "To a Letter-Carrier" and "At the Bar," with great gusto, the chuckling Williams insists: "I think that poetry comes out of the language that is spoken on the street."

The readings of the poems are always fascinating, even (late in life) when the frustrated poet repeats two or three times a poem that he has garbled. I count 145 different poems read on these tapes, some of them delivered several times on various occasions. "Listening to him read . . . makes clear the fundamental vocal origins of his development as a poet," notes Swigg in his essay. The voice served as a primary means of contact between the poet and the audience, a principle that shaped and directed Williams's writing from the beginning, when he involved himself in the editing and publication of the famous "little" magazine called *Contact*. It is a voice that riles, rouses, strokes, soothes, lulls, makes love to, seizes, and shakes the listener with the power of physical touch, making the body present in ways that are not possible for the page. "When you come to write, in the excitement of composition," he told an NBC interviewer in 1954, it inevitably comes out with whatever you hear, well, in your soul [he chuckles], if you wish to use such a term. It is a language which is variable and free. The language which we hear is the only language which carries conviction. When you're emotionally stirred, you don't pick and choose a scholastic language, but you speak with the emotions. That's what you're trying to do. And the emotions are things that follow a familiar pattern, and we want a familiar pattern, a home pattern, to bring the conviction to the listener."

Compassion was also at the core of Williams's philosophy. He told Mary Margaret McBride, who had asked him to define the physician's "bedside manner," that "you try to identify yourself with the person whom you're addressing. You try to be that person. . . . You are one with the person who you're treating" (tape 5). The ultimate contact is to become the other.

The sound quality of nearly all of the tapes is first-rate. When volume fluctuates, as it does in the Koehler tapes, Professor Swigg has supplied a transcript of the interview in the accompanying booklet. A complete reading of the first section of Williams's late masterpiece "Asphodel, That Greeny Flower" at the University of Puerto Rico in Mayagüez (the birthplace of his mother) is punctuated by tolling bells ("My enemies, the bells!" quips the poet) and twittering birds. The reading is oddly enhanced by the ravaged condition of the tape, especially an electronic microphone buzz that permeates the last minutes of the selection. It really sounds as if Williams is delivering the poem from some Beyond where bells toll, birds twitter, asphodels grow, and surrealist grid-noise permeates the landscape.

In his lectures Williams advances a number of ideas about poetry that are still vital. America has its own language that must be exploited by the poet ("Our life *isn't* Elizabethan," he asserts in one of his blistering attacks on iambic pentameter). All knowledge, not merely literary experience, presses into the composition of the poetic line, including the history of the American experiment, which (Williams is quoting Arnold Toynbee) came into existence "to make the benefits of civilization available for the whole human race." Liberated from the English tradition by Whitman, the American poet's line and how he shapes it reveals nothing less than "a new way . . . to organize society," since the poet "is a person living in a world which is unsatisfactory." Here Williams brings us right back to Plato: "The modes of music are never disturbed without

unsettling of the most fundamental political and social conventions. . . ."
He tells us in his lecture on "The Modern Poem" that the poem "is a cry
in the night. The night which surrounds us all. . . . It sprang from the
ground under my feet. It was associated with the *history*, and that was
of the ground which I was familiar with every day" (tape 12).

Williams became increasingly concerned about the technique of the
poem in his last two decades. Though Whitman had broken through to
a new expression with his free verse, Williams insisted that no verse is
"free." A new system of measuring the line had to be created, something
that he began to sense after he had written "The Descent" in 1947, in
which he first used the three-part (or three-ply) "stepped-down" line.
He invoked Einstein's Theory of Relativity, insisting that verse and measure follow mathematics: "The foot is to be taken relatively, relatively.
Not in the old method, but to be measured by a new standard which
will give us new control of the means of writing a poem" (tape 9).
Though Williams never quite pinned down his "variable foot" theory, his
ideas were picked up and developed by other poets, notably by Charles
Olson in his famous "Projective Verse" essay (1950). Williams reprinted
a good deal of it in his *Autobiography*, recognizing, perhaps, an advance
over his own thinking. Olson saw "projective verse" as a spontaneous
process: "It is right here, in the line, that the shaping takes place, each
moment of the going. . . ." And, "Already they [Pound and Williams] are
composing as though verse was to have the reading its writing involved,
as though not the eye but the ear was to be its measurer," stressing "the
full relevance of human voice . . . in the individual who writes." The
human breath, the human body made the measure. The measure—call it
the "variable foot," if you will—was there all those years, pumping
through that old erratic, idiosyncratic heart, so battered, but which in
these tapes pours its energy straight to us.

In their last interview (tape 10), Mary Margaret McBride asks
Williams, then seventy, the most irritating question an interviewer can
pose: that he "say something that'll live with everybody forever that you
found out about life. . . . What is it all about?" Williams replies,

> All I can say is *work*!—at what you choose as the finest thing that you
> know. Try to perfect yourself in that thing, and take your chances. "Cast
> thy bread on the waters." That's the one thing that has stood by me all my
> life. I don't have to take care of myself. Somebody else—and I'm not talking

transcendentally, either—but the world will take care of me plenty. All I have to do is do what I have to do, and let it go, carelessly. Let it go. Whatever happens to it, that's for somebody else to decide. Maybe I'll end up with my throat cut. Maybe it'll be due! But, if so, it's not for me to worry about it. *I don't care!* I have to do what I have to do, and that I'll do, right to the end, and I hope it'll be good.

Notes

1. *William Carlos Williams: The Collected Recordings*, tape 10.

2. William Carlos Williams, *I Wanted to Write a Poem: The Autobiography of the Works of a Poet*. Reported and edited by Edith Heal (New York: New Directions, revised edition, 1978), p. 4.

Gary Lenhart

A Brief Williams Chronology

1883   Born on September 17, in Rutherford, New Jersey, to William George Williams (an English citizen raised in the Caribbean) and Raquel Helène Rose Hoheb Williams (Puerto Rican and educated in Paris).

1897–99   Attends school in Switzerland.

1902–1906   Attends University of Pennsylvania to study medicine. Becomes friends with Ezra Pound, Hilda Doolittle (H. D.), and Charles Demuth.

1906–09   Interns at French and Child's Hospitals in New York City. Resigns from Child's Hospital rather than sign unauthenticated birth documents.

1909   Publication of first book, *Poems 1909*.

1910   Travels in Europe, then returns to begin practice of medicine in Rutherford.

1912   Marries Florence ("Flossie") Herman.

1913   Armory Show in NYC. Pound arranges for WCW's second book of poems, *The Tempers*, to be published by Elkin Mathews in London.

1914   Birth of first son, William Eric. Begins association with Alfred Kreymborg and *Others* group.

1916   Birth of second son, Paul Herman.

1917	Publication of *Al que quiere!*
1920	*Kora in Hell* published. With Robert McAlmon, edits the little magazine *Contact*, which they continue to publish until 1923.
1923	*Spring and All* and *The Great American Novel* published.
1924	WCW takes sabbatical from his medical practice. He and Flossie travel in Europe, spending much time in Paris, where he meets Gertrude Stein, James Joyce, Ernest Hemingway, and others.
1925	*In the American Grain* published.
1927	Receives *The Dial* Award. Uses it to settle libel suit resulting from publication of short story "The Five Dollar Guy" in *The New Masses*. Travels to Europe with family. Wife and son remain in Switzerland, where sons attend school for the year.
1928	Publication of *A Voyage to Pagany*.
1930	Agrees to edit new magazine, *Pagany*, with Richard Johns. Continues until 1932.
1932	*The Knife of the Times* and *A Novelette and Other Prose* published. *Contact* magazine is revived, with Nathanael West as Williams's co-editor.
1934	*The Collected Poems (1921–31)* published, with preface by Wallace Stevens.
1937	Harvard undergraduate James Laughlin publishes *White Mule* (first volume of the Stecher trilogy) as first New Directions book.

1938	*Life Along the Passaic River* (stories) and *The Complete Collected Poems* published.
1940	*In the Money* (vol. 2 of the Stecher trilogy) published.
1944	After being turned down by New Directions and several other publishers who blamed the wartime paper shortage, Williams finds a small press to publish *The Wedge*.
1946	Publication of first book of *Paterson*. With good reviews, Williams is "discovered" by the mainstream literary press.
1948	Publication of *Paterson, Book Two* and *A Dream of Love* (play). Williams suffers first heart attack.
1949	Death of Williams's mother. Publication of *The Pink Church*, *Selected Poems*, and *Paterson, Book Three*.
1950	Wins National Book Award for *Paterson*. Publishes *Collected Later Poems* and *Make Light of It* (stories).
1951	Publishes *Autobiography*, *The Collected Earlier Poems*, and *Paterson, Book Four*. Suffers first major stroke.
1952	Suffers another serious stroke. Publishes final volume of the Stecher trilogy, *The Build-Up*.
1954	Publication of *The Desert Music* and *Selected Essays*.
1955	Publishes *Journey to Love*.
1957	Publishes *Selected Letters*.
1958	Publishes *I Wanted to Write a Poem* and *Paterson, Book Five*. Suffers third major stroke.
1959	Publication of *Yes, Mrs. Williams*. *Many Loves* produced off-Broadway.

1961   *The Farmers' Daughters* (collected stories) and *Many Loves and Other Plays* published. More debilitating strokes.

1962   *Pictures from Brueghel* published, to quiet reception.

1963   Dies on March 4. Pulitzer Prize awarded posthumously.

Williams Resources

Editions

The Autobiography of William Carlos Williams. New York: New Directions, 1967. Hastily written to deadline, full of errors and edited through the eye of memory, this book estranged friends and riled enemies. But it does capture the spirit of WCW's poetic adventure.

The Build-Up. New York: New Directions, 1968. The concluding volume of the Stecher trilogy. Joe's successful business allows the family to move to suburban New Jersey and build the "mansion" his wife has always wanted.

The Collected Poems of William Carlos Williams, Volume I: 1909-1939. New York: New Directions, 1986. Edited by A. Walton Litz and Christopher MacGowan. *The Collected Poems of William Carlos Williams, Volume II: 1939-1962.* New York: New Directions, 1988. Edited by Christopher MacGowan. These are the standard editions of the poet's work. They include helpful notes, group the poems into the books in which they were originally published, and supplement them with unpublished and discarded poems. The design is not as attractive as that of the volumes they replace (*Collected Earlier* and *Collected Later*), which gave respectful room to all poems. Here they are cheek to jowl, as in a Norton anthology. As a result, however, they are reasonably priced and comprehensive. Very highly recommended.

The Collected Stories. New York: New Directions 1996. Introduction by Sherwin B. Nuland. Formerly *The Farmers' Daughters.*

The Doctor Stories. New York: New Directions 1984. This volume includes thirteen stories about doctoring selected from *The Farmers' Daughters*, the chapter from the *Autobiography* titled "The Practice," and six poems about practicing medicine.

The Embodiment of Knowledge. New York: New Directions, 1974. In this book, written hastily at a time when WCW was frustrated with the schooling of his sons, Williams tries to distinguish knowledge from pedantry, using Shakespeare as his touchstone. He never published the manuscript, which has been carefully reconstructed from Williams's papers by Ron Loewinsohn.

The Farmers' Daughters: The Collected Stories. New York: New Directions, 1961, 1980. Includes 52 stories previously published in *The Knife of the Times*, *Life Along the Passaic River*, and *Make Light of It*, and the long story "The Farmers' Daughters." Reprinted as *The Collected Stories of William Carlos Williams*.

I Wanted to Write a Poem: The Autobiography of the Works of the Poet, reported and edited by Edith Heal. New York: New Directions, 1978. Edith Heal interviewed WCW and Flossie to create this little annotated bibiliography. The result has the flavor of memory—sometimes failing, but sparked by what stays. Recommended.

Imaginations. New York: New Directions, 1971. Reprints in one volume five early and out-of-print books: *Kora in Hell, Spring and All, The Descent of Winter, The Great American Novel*, and *A Novelette & Other Prose*. The zest of the experimental still vivifies this collection.

In the American Grain. New York: New Directions, 1956. A peculiar look at the Americas from the time of Red Eric to Abraham Lincoln in a series of essays about individual figures and episodes. WCW transcribed three chapters from documents, wrote the chapter on Aaron Burr from Flossie's dictation, and composed the rest in excited, sometimes difficult prose. One of the great strange books of the century. Highly recommended.

In the Money. New York: New Directions, 1968. Volume Two in the Stecher trilogy tells of immigrant Joe Stecher's struggle to establish his printing business.

Kora in Hell: Improvisations. San Francisco: City Lights, 1957. First published in a limited edition, this book had been unavailable for thirty years when City Lights published it in its series of contemporary avant-garde poetry. This edition is out of print again, but fortunately *Kora in Hell* is included in *Imaginations*.

Last Nights of Paris by Philippe Soupault. New York: Full Court Press, 1982; Cambridge, Mass.: Exact Change, 1992. Translated by William Carlos Williams. Williams met Soupault in Paris in 1924, and upon his return translated this novel of the nocturnal Paris underworld with the aid of his mother.

Many Loves and Other Plays. New York: New Directions, 1965. Theater was one of the poet's early loves, and he continued to write plays throughout his life. Some scripts were lost, others apparently discarded. This collects those he wished and was able to preserve.

Paterson, edited by Christopher MacGowan. New York: New Directions, 1995. WCW's epic, in five books with notes for a sixth. MacGowan again supplies extensive helpful notes.

Pictures from Brueghel: Collected Poems 1950–1962 . New York: New Directions, 1963. WCW's last book, including "Asphodel, That Greeny Flower" and other poems composed with the triadic line he first came to in "The Descent." These poems are included in *The Collected Poems, Volume II*, but it's nice to have them in this handy edition.

A Recognizable Image: William Carlos Williams on Art and Artists. New York: New Directions, 1979. Edited, with an introduction and notes, by Bram Dijkstra. WCW's mother was a painter, as a young man he also painted, and several times he commented that painting had made an enormous impact on his art. He remained friends throughout his life with the artists Charles Demuth, Charles Sheeler, and Marsden Hartley. This volume collects his published essays on individual artists, paintings, and exhibitions, and includes previously unpublished articles on the visual arts.

Selected Essays. New York: Random House, 1954; New York: New Directions, 1969. Because the selection was made by WCW, we can see what statements he was particularly eager to preserve, including "Prologue to *Kora in Hell*," "A Matisse," "The American Background: America and Alfred Stieglitz," "Introduction to *The Wedge*," and two essays each on Gertrude Stein, Marianne Moore, and Ezra Pound.

The Selected Letters of William Carlos Williams. New York: MacDowell, Obolensky, 1957; New York: New Directions, 1984. A judicious and spare selection from a prolific correspondent, this volume extends through 1956. Though illness curbed WCW's letter writing after that date, we could still use an expanded edition, perhaps even a multi-volume collected letters.

Selected Poems. New York: New Directions, 1985. Edited by Charles Tomlinson. Unfortunately, this has replaced the out-of-print selection made by WCW himself in 1948 and updated by "editorial advisors" in 1968. Tomlinson favors the strictly imagist and "objectivist" poems, and his selection distorts the view of Williams in that direction.

Something to Say: William Carlos Williams on Younger Poets. New York: New Directions, 1985. Edited by James E.B. Breslin. A collection of essays about poets younger than WCW, including several reprinted from the *Selected Essays*. Among the writers covered in this volume are George Oppen, Louis Zukofsky, Marcia Nardi, Norman MacLeod, Kenneth Patchen, Allen Ginsberg, Muriel Rukeyser, and Kenneth Rexroth.

A Vogage to Pagany. New York: New Directions, 1970. Protagonist Dr. Evans, who closely resembles the author, travels to Europe. Includes pages adapted from WCW's European diary.

White Mule. New York: New Directions, 1967. This first novel in the Stecher trilogy, which relates the saga of Flossie's family in America, remains the best. The pages dealing with the birth of the heroine are among the most extraordinary portraits of a baby in literature.

Yes, Mrs. Williams. New York: New Directions, 1975. Before it was first published in 1959, WCW struggled on and off for more than 20 years with this portrait of his elderly mother. Though the poet remained dissatisfied with the result, it is a surprising and magical little gift. Recommended highly to WCW fans, cautiously to others.

Letters

Williams was a prolific letter writer. In addition to the *Selected Letters*, several volumes of his correspondence with individual writers have been published.

The Last Word: Letters Between Marcia Nardi and William Carlos Williams, edited by Elizabeth M. O'Neil. Iowa City: University of Iowa,

1994. Poet Marcia Nardi was the young woman whose letters Williams included in *Paterson*, giving her the pseudonym Cress.

Selected Letters of Ezra Pound and William Carlos Williams. New York: New Directions, 1995. Pound was WCW's dear friend, energetic sponsor, and arrogant nemesis for sixty years. Their letters reveal a course of loyal friendship even rockier than most.

William Carlos Williams and James Laughlin: Selected Letters, edited by Hugh Witemeyer. New York: Norton, 1989. While still a Harvard undergraduate, Laughlin launched New Directions with the publication of *White Mule* in 1937. He continued as Williams's publisher and friend until the poet's death.

William Carlos Williams/John Sanford: A Correspondence. Oyster Press, Santa Barbara, 1984. When this brief correspondence begins in 1932, Sanford is still Julian Shapiro, an aspiring young novelist and friend of Nathanael West whose stories were published in *Contact*. It ends in 1950, with Williams promising to recommend Sanford's novel to New Directions.

Biographies

Baldwin, Neil. *To All Gentleness: Williams Carlos Williams, The Doctor Poet*. New York: Atheneum, 1984. A concise, lucid, heroic biography addressed to younger readers. Baldwin catalogued the major Williams collection at Buffalo's Lockwood Library, and knows his subject intimately. With a foreword by William Eric Williams and some of the best Williams family photographs to have been published.

Laughlin, James. *Remembering William Carlos Williams*. New York: New Directions, 1995. This slim volume, composed in a narrative meter adapted from Kenneth Rexroth, recounts with astounding candor the sometimes stormy relations between Williams and his publisher over the last twenty-seven years of the doctor's life. Though Laughlin has little to say about Williams as artist that's not heard elsewhere, this could serve as a useful introduction to the writer.

Mariani, Paul. *William Carlos Williams: A New World Naked*. New York: McGraw-Hill, 1981. Energetic, inclusive (874 pages), and reliable, this is the five-star biography for Williams enthusiasts. The index is thorough and helpful. I consulted this book frequently during the preparation of this edition, and acknowledge a particular debt to it in assembling the brief chronology that appears here. Indispensable for anyone interested in Williams's life.

Weaver, Mike. *William Carlos Williams: The American Background.* London: Cambridge University Press, 1971. The next best thing to Mariani's biography, and one-fourth the length. Weaver provides the social and intellectual context for WCW's effort. Though Weaver's strokes are of necessity broad, this remains a useful companion to reading Williams. Includes a selection from Thomas Ward's long 1842 poem "Passaic" and helpful "Notes to Paterson."

Whittemore, Reed. *William Carlos Williams: Poet from Jersey.* Boston: Houghton Mifflin, 1975. According to William Eric Williams, Whittemore was Flossie Williams's choice to write her husband's biography. But Whittemore lacked conviction for the job. His condescension toward his subject is sure to anger Williams loyalists.

Criticism

Coles, Robert. *William Carlos Williams: The Knack of Survival in America.* New Brunswick, N.J.: Rutgers University Press, 1975. Lectures by the editor of *The Doctor Stories* about Williams's short stories and novels.

Frail, David. *The Early Politics and Poetics of William Carlos Williams.* Ann Arbor, Mich.: UMI Research Press, 1987. Provides a very clear background for the early poems, with excellent notes and bibliography.

Kenner, Hugh. *A Homemade World.* New York: Knopf, 1975; *The Pound Era.* Berkeley: University of California Press, 1971. These books are not specifically about Williams, but American modernist poetry. Still, the comments on Williams (mentioned throughout the first; in *The Pound Era* in chapters "Syntax in Rutherford" and "The Jersey Paideuma") remain among the most lucid, concise critical analyses of Williams's achievement.

Mariani, Paul. *William Carlos Williams: The Poet and His Critics.* Chicago: American Library Association, 1975. Mariani deserves further gratitude for thoroughly researching and summarizing all known reviews of Williams before 1973. Williams was critically neglected until in his mid-sixties, but neglect may have been preferable to some of the few reviews he did receive. But there are lighter moments, as when Baroness Elsa von Freytag-Loringhoven published a two-part review of *Kora in Hell* titled "Thee I Call 'Hamlet of Wedding-Ring.'"

Marzán, Julio. *The Spanish American Roots of William Carlos Williams*. Austin: University of Texas Press, 1994. Explores the impact on Williams's writing of his Spanish American heritage. For too many years, this aspect of Williams's background was neglected. Victor Hernández Cruz has published a fine essay on the same subject ("Encounters with an Americano Poet: William Carlos Williams " in *Conjunctions 29*, published by Bard College).

Miller, J. Hillis, ed. *William Carlos Williams: A Collection of Critical Essays*. Englewood Cliffs, N.J.: Prentice Hall, 1966. A convenient gathering of opinions by Williams's peers. Published shortly after Williams's death, with essays by Ezra Pound, Marianne Moore, Kenneth Burke, Wallace Stevens, Robert Lowell, Robert Creeley, and others.

Sorrentino, Gilbert. *Something Said*. San Francisco: North Point, 1984. Between 1962 and 1983, Sorrentino published seven trenchant essays on Williams (including a review of Mariani's biography) that promoted him as forerunner of what Sorrentino considered a mid-century American poetic revolution. They comprise thirty-six pages of this collection.

Tashjian, Dickran. *William Carlos Williams and the American Scene 1920–1940*. New York: Whitney Museum of American Art in association with the University of California Press, 1978. The catalogue for an exhibition of twenty years of American painting that locates Williams among the included visual artists. Nearly half the scholarly books written about Williams have to do with his relation to the visual arts. Though twenty years old, this catalogue remains the best introduction to that side of Williams—not least because it has the best reproductions. The range of art, from Cubism and Dada to folk and proletarian, reflects the breadth of WCW's artistic interests.

William Carlos Williams: Man and Poet, edited with an introduction by Carroll Terrell. Orono, Me.: National Poetry Foundation/University of

Maine at Orono, 1983. This 617-page tome was published to celebrate WCW's 100th birthday. Despite the academic filler, it would be worth reading *in toto* for the twenty-two-page essay "Life with Father" by William Eric Williams. It also includes an essay by Allen Ginsberg, an interview with Robert Creeley, and good essays by Mary Barnard, John G. Dollar, Ezra Pound, Marjorie Perloff, Denise Levertov, Ron Loewinsohn, and Gilbert Sorrentino.

Wagner, Linda Welshimer. *The Poems of William Carlos Williams: A Critical Study*. Middletown, Conn.: Wesleyan University Press, 1964. *The Prose of William Carlos Williams*. Middletown, Conn.: Wesleyan University Press, 1970. Wagner, who also edited a book of interviews with Williams, discusses his poetry and prose as one art united by its insistence on the American idiom, the local, and organic form.

Wallace, Emily. *A Bibliography of William Carlos Williams*. Middletown, Conn.: Wesleyan University Press, 1968. Thirty years old, but still the standard bibliography for works published during the poet's lifetime.

Zukofsky, Louis. *Prepositions: The Collected Critical Essays*. Berkeley: University of California Press, 1981. For thirty years, WCW relied on Zukofsky to read and edit his work, and rarely demurred at his suggested changes. The first essay about WCW in this volume was written in 1928, the last in 1958.

Magazines

William Carlos Williams Review. With subscriptions currently at the bargain rate of $15/year for individuals, $20/year for institutions, it's worth every penny, and with your subscription you become a member of the William Carlos Williams Society. In addition to scholarly articles and notes about WCW, there are book reviews and a current bibliography. Checks should be made out to the *William Carlos Williams Review* and mailed to *William Carlos Williams Review,* Brian Bremen, Editor, Department of English, University of Texas, Austin, TX 78712-1164.

Sagetrieb: A Journal Devoted to Poets in the Imagist/Objectivist Tradition. The "Imagist/Objectivist tradition" seems too narrow to hold the protean WCW, but the National Poetry Foundation does such devoted scholarly work that I don't want to quibble. The subtitle used to be *A*

Journal Devoted to Poets in the Pound-H.D.-Williams Tradition. There is a 1998 double issue on "William Carlos Williams and Language." Address: 305 Neville Hall, University of Maine at Orono, Orono, Maine 04469.

Films, Videotapes, Audiotapes, and Interviews

See Bill Zavatsky's article in this book, pp. 163–174.

Internet

The World Wide Web address for *The William Carlos Williams Review* and the William Carlos Williams Society is http://www.en.utexas/~wcw.

Notes on Contributors

JULIA ALVAREZ is the author of three novels, *How the García Girls Lost Their Accents, In the Time of the Butterflies,* and *¡Yo!,* as well as two books of poems, *Homecoming* and *The Other Side.* She has taught creative writing to students and teachers at all levels, most recently at Middlebury College in Vermont.

BOB BLAISDELL teaches writing and literature at Kingsborough Community College in Brooklyn. He edited *Hardy's Selected Poetry* and *"The Fiddler of the Reel" and Other Stories,* both published by Dover Books.

REED BYE received a doctorate in English Literature from the University of Colorado. He is the author of five books of poetry, most recently *Passing Freaks and Graces* (Rodent Press). Bye is currently Chair of the Department of Writing and Poetics at The Naropa Institute in Boulder, Colorado.

SALLY COBAU received her M.F.A. in creative writing from the University of Montana. Since 1995 she has taught writing in grades 1–12 with the Missoula Writing Collaborative. In addition, she originated a middle school girls' writing workshop and a summer poetry camp. Cobau has had poems published in *LitRag* and has read her work on Montana Public Radio.

BARBARA FLUG COLIN has been Writer in Residence at the Henry Viscardi School in Albertson, New York, since 1989. Her writing has appeared in *Arts, New York Arts Journal, Art Now, M/e/a/n/i/n/g, New Observations,* and *Teachers & Writers.* Recently she completed a novella, *The Genealogy of Sport.*

JORDAN DAVIS's books of poetry include *Upstairs* and *Poem on a Train,* both published by Barque Press. With Anna Malmude he hosts the Poetry City reading series at Teachers & Writers Collaborative. For several years he has taught writing at the School for the Physical City in New York.

CHRISTOPHER EDGAR is a writer, translator, editor, and teacher. He coedited *Educating the Imagination, Old Faithful,* and *The Nearness of You: Students and Teachers Writing On-line,* all published by Teachers & Writers. He teaches poetry at the School for the Physical City in New York, and is Editor at Teachers & Writers Collaborative.

PEGGY GARRISON received an M.A. in creative writing from The City University of New York. She has been teaching poetry in public schools since 1976. She also teaches creative writing at New York University. In 1993 Garrison received the New York City Arts in Education Round-table Award for Sustained Achievement in Literature. Her work has appeared in *The Literary Review, Beloit Fiction Journal, Teachers & Writers, The Village Voice,* and many other magazines.

Poet ALLEN GINSBERG (1926–1997) was a mentor for generations of young Americans, as Williams had been a mentor for him. In 1984, Harper & Row published Ginsberg's *Collected Poems.*

PENNY HARTER is the author of fifteen books of poems, most recently *Lizard Light: Poems from the Earth* (Sherman Asher Publishing). She has received awards from the N.J. State Council on the Arts, the Geraldine R. Dodge Foundation, and the Poetry Society of America. She and her husband, the poet and translator William J. Higginson, live in Santa Fe, N.M., where she teaches English at Santa Fe Preparatory School.

KENNETH KOCH has published many books of poetry, drama, and fiction, as well as classic guides to writing poetry. His most recent books are *Straits* (Knopf), *Selected Poems 1950–1988* (Knopf), *I Never Told Anybody* (new edition, Teachers & Writers), *The Art of Poetry* (University of Michigan), and *Making Your Own Days* (Scribner). Koch is Professor of English at Columbia University.

GARY LENHART, the editor of the present volume, is also a poet and teacher. His books include *One at a Time* (United Artists), *Light Heart,* and *Father and Son Night* (both from Hanging Loose). Lenhart edited two literary magazines, *Mag City* and *Transfer,* as well as *The Selected Poems of Michael Scholnick.* He teaches creative writing and college composition in Vermont.

CHARLES NORTH's most recent books are *The Year of the Olive Oil* (poems) and *No Other Way: Selected Prose*, both from Hanging Loose Press. Forthcoming from Sun & Moon is his *New & Selected Poems*. North is Poet in Residence at Pace College in New York.

RON PADGETT's most recent books are *Creative Reading* (NCTE) and *New & Selected Poems* (Godine). The University of California published his translation of *The Complete Poems* of Blaise Cendrars. Padgett is Publications Director at Teachers & Writers Collaborative, for whom he edited the *Handbook of Poetic Forms*. He teaches imaginative writing at Columbia University.

DAVID SURFACE is a fiction writer, essayist, and teacher. He has taught as a writer-in-the-schools for the Lincoln Center Department of Education and currently leads fiction workshops for adults at the Hudson Valley Writers' Center. His fiction and essays have appeared in *North American Review*, *DoubleTake*, *Crazyhorse*, *Fiction*, *Artful Dodge*, and the *Marlboro Review*. He lives in Brooklyn, New York.

MARY EDWARDS WERTSCH, the author of *Military Brats: Legacies of Childhood inside the Fortress*, is primarily a writer of nonfiction. Her passion for teaching poetry writing to children was born in 1994, after reading two books published by Teachers & Writers. She has been teaching ever since, primarily through St. Louis's Springboard to Learning program.

BILL ZAVATSKY is a poet, translator, editor, and teacher. His books include *Theories of Rain* and *The Whole Word Catalogue 2,* as well as translations of Valery Larbaud's *Poems of A. O. Barnabooth* and André Breton's *Earthlight: Poems*, which won the 1993 PEN/Book-of-the-Month Club Translation Prize. Zavatsky teaches high school English at Trinity School in New York City.

OTHER T&W BOOKS YOU MIGHT ENJOY

The T&W Guide to Walt Whitman, edited by Ron Padgett. The first and only guide to teaching the work of Walt Whitman from K–college. "A lively, fun, illuminating book"—Ed Folsom, editor of The Walt Whitman Quarterly.

The T&W Guide to Frederick Douglass, edited by Wesley Brown, provides a variety of ways for students to experience Douglass' Narrative as an aesthetic achievement as well as a socio-historical document. "An impressive collection, well written . . . solid and very usable . . . particularly inspiring"—Contemparary Education.

The Teachers & Writers Handbook of Poetic Forms, edited by Ron Padgett. This T&W bestseller includes 74 entries on traditional and modern poetic forms by 19 poet-teachers. "A treasure"—Kliatt. "The definitions not only inform, they often provoke and inspire. A small wonder!"—Poetry Project Newsletter. "An entertaining reference work"—Teaching English in the Two-Year College. "A solid beginning reference source"—Choice.

Poetry Everywhere: Teaching Poetry Writing in School and in the Community by Jack Collom and Sheryl Noethe. This big and "tremendously valuable resource work for teachers" (Kliatt) at all levels contains 60 writing exercises, extensive commentary, and 450 examples.

Luna, Luna: Creative Writing Ideas from Spanish, Latin American, & Latino Literature, edited by Julio Marzán. In 21 lively and practical essays, poets, fiction writers, and teachers tell how they use the work of Lorca, Neruda, Jiménez, Cisneros, and others to inspire students to write imaginatively. Luna, Luna "succeeds brilliantly. I highly recommend this book: it not only teaches but guides teachers on how to involve students in the act of creative writing"—Kliatt.

Sing the Sun Up: Creative Writing Ideas from African American Literature, edited by Lorenzo Thomas. Twenty teaching writers present new and exciting ways to motivate students to write imaginatively, inspired by African American poetry, fiction, essays, and drama. Essays in the book discuss work by James Baldwin, Gwendolyn Brooks, Zora Neale Hurston, Jean Toomer, Aimé Césaire, Countee Cullen, Lucille Clifton, Jayne Cortez, Rita Dove, and others.

The Story in History: Writing Your Way into the American Experience by Margot Fortunato Galt. "One of the best idea books for teachers I have ever read. . . . Rich lodes of writing ideas. . . . This is a book that can make a difference"—Kliatt.

Educating the Imagination, Vols. 1 & 2, edited by Christopher Edgar and Ron Padgett. A huge selection of the best articles from 17 years of Teachers & Writers magazine, with ideas and assignments for writing poetry, fiction, plays, history, folklore, parodies, and much more.

Old Faithful: 18 Writers Present Their Favorite Writing Assignments, edited by Christopher Edgar and Ron Padgett. A collection of sure-fire exercises in imaginative writing for all levels, developed and tested by veteran writing teachers.

·

For a complete free T&W publications catalogue, contact
Teachers & Writers Collaborative
5 Union Square West, New York, NY 10003-3306
tel. (toll-free) 888-BOOKS-TW
Visit our World Wide Web site at http://www.twc.org